I0799240

What people are saying about ...

FAKE ID

"I found this book both fascinating and of great benefit. Abdu helps us understand the conflict between humanity and AI, the complexity of technology, and how it will be used to define what it means to be human. Where do we turn when reality collapses and we no longer know who we are? Why must we return to a biblical view of mankind to keep our sanity in the midst of our confused world? Be better prepared for a future that is already here: *Read this book!*"

Pastor Erwin Lutzer, pastor emeritus of Moody Church, Chicago

"Perhaps the biggest deception in all of recorded history is Satan's lie that we, rather than God, define what it means to be a human being. This was the lie that led to Adam and Eve's original sin. This was the lie of gnosticism in the first century Church. And this is the lie of the LGBTQIA tsunami overwhelming all of Western civilization. Abdu Murray brings a much-needed dose of truth to this debate. You must read this book."

Everett Piper, PhD, president emeritus of Oklahoma Wesleyan University, bestselling author of *Not a Daycare*, columnist for the Washington Times, radio host and speaker

"At the root of every cultural confusion we face is a crisis. It's not fundamentally a moral crisis, though we'll have to make difficult decisions in the days ahead. Fundamentally, we face an anthropological crisis. And just as we've forgotten who we are and what makes us humans, our technologies have made it possible to try things previous generations could not have imagined. We are desperate for clarity, and Abdu Murray has provided much of it in this book. *Fake ID* could not have come to us at a better time."

John Stonestreet, host of *Breakpoint* and co-author of *A Practical Guide to Culture*

"Evolutionary man lives under the illusion that what God is, man may become. This aptly sums up the reality collapse that noted worldview apologist Abdu Murray addresses in *Fake ID*. Not content to curse the darkness, Murray provides a lighthouse amid the gathering storm. This book offers a mega-shift in perception from buying the materialist myth that artificial intelligence is akin to actual intelligence and contrasts biological realities with biotic myth."

Hank Hanegraaff, president of the Christian Research Institute, host of the *Bible Answer Man* broadcast and the *Hank Unplugged* podcast, and author of many books, including *MUSLIM: What You Need to Know About the World's Fastest-Growing Religion*

"Are humans just meat-based machines? Is our identity entirely fluid, purely determined by our own whims and feelings? Or is there something deeper that it means to be human? In *Fake ID*, Abdu

Murray tackles these contemporary questions with courage and conviction, showing that the timeless message of Jesus has much to say about our culture's current confusion about reality."

Andy Bannister, director of Solas and author of *How to Talk About Jesus Without Looking Like an Idiot* and *The Atheist Who Didn't Exist*

"I cannot think of a timelier book than Abdu Murray's *Fake ID.* This is a thought-provoking and deeply insightful exploration of the cultural forces shaping our understanding of identity and reality in the age of AI and post-truth ideologies. The author masterfully combines philosophical rigor, scientific analysis, and spiritual wisdom to address the profound challenges posed by Bioclasm and AI-Mania. With compelling arguments and compassionate truth-telling, this book offers a hopeful vision for rediscovering what it means to be human, grounded in the timeless wisdom of the imago Dei. Accept this invitation to embrace truth, dignity, and purpose in a rapidly changing world. A must-read for anyone seeking clarity and direction amidst the cultural chaos."

Juan Valdes, DMin, apologist, international conference speaker, and author of *How to Think: A Crash Course in Critical Thinking*

"Abdu Murray eloquently exposes the grave dangers to humanity of the current exponential advances of Bioclasm—the denial of biological reality—and AI-Mania—the denial that humans are more than physical entities. Murray shows how these denials of reality give us a rare and powerful opportunity to prove human exceptionalism and the Christian doctrine of humans as the unique bearers of the image of God."

Hugh Ross, astronomer and founder of Reasons to Believe

"While Abdu didn't intend for *Fake ID* to be a parenting book, it is in fact one of the most important parenting books of the decade. Abdu writes with clarity, relatability, and brilliance. Every parent who cares enough to help their kids navigate a confusing and often toxic culture *must* read *Fake ID*."

Meg Meeker, MD, author, pediatrician

FAKE ID

How AI and Identity Ideology Are Collapsing Reality—and What to Do About It

ABDU MURRAY

150 YEARS STRONG
DAVID C COOK

FAKE ID
Published by David C Cook
4050 Lee Vance Drive
Colorado Springs, CO 80918 U.S.A.

Integrity Music Limited, a Division of David C Cook
Brighton, East Sussex BN1 2RE, England

Library of Congress Control Number 2025943022
ISBN 978-0-8307-8949-8
eISBN 978-0-8307-8950-4

The Team: Luke McKinnon, Jeff Gerke, Gina Pottenger,
Dana Carrington, Susan Murdock
Cover Design: Micah Kandros

Printed in the United States of America
First Edition 2026

1 2 3 4 5 6 7 8 9 10

103125

For Dad. I miss you deeply.

CONTENTS

Prologue

BETWEEN REALITY AND COLLAPSE

We stand at a precipice of history—not because our technologies have brought us to the brink of destruction nor because our social developments threaten civilization itself. Rather, the precariousness stems from how two powerful cultural tsunamis are crashing against our shared understanding of reality.

The first tsunami, which I call *Bioclasm*, pushes us to subordinate biological (e.g., gender) reality to subjective feelings about identity. The second, which I term *AI-Mania*, pulls us toward uncritical reliance on artificial intelligence, where deepfakes and humanesque abilities have the potential to erode our ability to understand what makes us uniquely human.

This book is not meant to be a "doomer" diatribe. Nor am I offering a wholesale rejection of technological advancement. I am something of a technophile myself, appreciating the genuine benefits that artificial intelligence brings to health care, research, accessibility, and countless other fields. And I must be clear that my criticisms of identity ideologies are not aimed at those who suffer with genuinely diagnosable gender dysphoria. Gender dysphoria is a painful psychological condition in which a person's mental impression of their gender doesn't match their biological sex. I have tried to approach the issue from science and logic and informed by truths of the Christian faith. People who experience genuine gender dysphoria deserve compassion, dignity, and respect—not derision.

A friend encapsulated two ways people with opposing views approach caring for those with gender dysphoria. Those who affirm transgenderism focus their care on changing a person's body to match the mind (by means of surgery, hormone replacement, etc.). Those who do not affirm transgenderism care by focusing on changing the suffering individual's mind to match the body. There are those on both sides of this issue who sincerely care about the well-being of those who suffer. While I strongly believe that changing the body and blurring the essential distinctions between the two biological sexes are dangerously wrong, I'm trying not to criticize anyone's sincerity. But sincerity uncoupled from truth won't help anyone.

What I am critiquing are ideologies, not individuals, especially ideologies that pretend to care for the well-being of others while they actually use people to advance an agenda. These ideologies, when taken to extremes, cause us to lose sight of what is real and what matters.

The phrase *reality collapse* first caught my attention during a discussion between AI researchers Tristan Harris and Aza Raskin.[1] Though they mentioned it only briefly, the concept lingered in my mind, eventually crystallizing my concerns about our post-truth cultural moment. In such a moment, when preferences matter more than facts and truth, we are particularly susceptible to reality collapse—the inability to discern the authentic from the artificial.

Bioclasm—the ideology that elevates subjective feelings over biological reality and demands universal affirmation of those feelings—collapses reality through social coercion. "Identity contains the good and ill of all 'isms,'" Jonathan Pageau notes, "and it is bound up in all positions of authority and social functions at different scales in a social body, or even authority within our own minds."[2] Bioclasm doesn't merely allow people to identify differently—it demands that everyone affirm those identities, even when they contradict observable reality. It isn't just a cultural shift; it's a revolution in how we define personhood itself, and it carries with it the power to silence dissent, punish truth-telling, and collapse shared reality.

This is distinct from acknowledging genuine gender dysphoria and having compassion for those who suffer through it. Bioclasm is its own form of fundamentalism. According to Jens Zimmermann, "Fundamentalism," whether religious or secular, "hates complexity, is impatient with ambiguity, remains blind to the historical development of its own position and likes to create totalizing views of reality. Fundamentalism refuses to grant legitimacy to dimensions of human experience that challenge its own worldview."[3] Compassion, to be genuine, sometimes has to risk upsetting fundamentalists because neither society writ large nor individuals can afford comforting fictions.

In contrast, AI-Mania collapses reality through seduction rather than coercion. The more we rely on artificial intelligence to curate our information, create our content, and even simulate our relationships, the more we risk diminishing our own agency and creativity. When algorithms predict our preferences so accurately that we no longer need to discover them for ourselves, when algorithms stoke the flames of radicalization, when AI can generate essays, images, and music that we claim as our own, something essential about human creativity, compassion, and authenticity begins to fade.

I understand the allure of both these forces. As someone of Arab descent and a former Muslim and now a Christian, I recognize how tempting it is to build my identity primarily around ethnic or religious markers. When Middle Eastern conflicts flare, I feel the tug of ethnic solidarity. When religious differences arise, I feel the pull of old allegiances. Those markers are incredibly important, of course. But they are not definitional. If I remain fixed on these aspects of my identity, I risk collapsing under the weight of my biases the complex reality of what's actually happening in the world. Similarly, as someone who values efficiency and innovation, I'm drawn to technologies that promise to make life easier, more productive, and more connected. Yet I've also experienced moments of disorientation when AI generates content that seems eerily humanlike.

The consequences of reality collapse are not merely philosophical. When we lose our shared commitment to truth, we lose our ability to collaborate, to build consensus, and to solve problems. When identity becomes the primary lens through which we view the world, we fragment into increasingly isolated tribes. When we outsource our thinking and creating to machines, we risk atrophying the very faculties that make us human.

We need compassionate truth-telling. When reality collapses, human flourishing suffers. To discuss these issues rightly, we need a way that neither demonizes those with whom we disagree nor abandons our commitment to truth. This middle path—one that refuses the false choice between harsh judgment and uncritical affirmation—is what I hope to chart in the pages that follow. To the extent that I veer from that path, I ask forgiveness and hope to be corrected.

Yet this book isn't merely a warning; it's an invitation to rediscover what it means to be human while we stand on the precipice of reality collapse. It's an appeal to find meaning not in the malleable clay of our self-created identities but in the givenness of our embodied essences. It's a call to use technology as a tool rather than allowing it to use us. My goal is neither alarmism nor resignation but a clear-eyed assessment of our cultural moment and a hopeful vision for navigating it with wisdom and grace.

Throughout these pages, I'll argue that the antidote to reality collapse isn't found in rejecting technological progress or in dismissing the complexity of human identity. Rather, it's found in recovering a vision of humanity grounded in truth, in seeing ourselves as neither mere machines nor gods of our own making but as bearers of the divine image with both limits and transcendent potential.

As we navigate the tsunamis of Bioclasm and AI-Mania, we need a sextant—a navigational tool to help us find our bearings when landmarks disappear. My contention is that such a sextant exists in the timeless wisdom that informs us about what it means to be human:

beings created in God's image yet bounded by the realities of our physical existence.

As we begin this exploration together, I invite you to approach these pages not with defensiveness but with openness, not looking for confirmation of what you already believe but for insight into our shared human condition. For it is only by understanding the forces that threaten to collapse reality that we can hope to strengthen it.

Chapter One

REALITY COLLAPSE

There Are Four Lights

"There! Are! Four! Lights!"

Captain Jean-Luc Picard pushed these words through tortured vocal cords, his voice barely rising above a hoarse whisper. In an iconic episode of *Star Trek: The Next Generation*, Picard has been captured and tortured for weeks by a man bent on breaking his spirit. Picard's enemy has implanted a device in his body capable of delivering unimaginable pain at the push of a button. The torturer turns on a set of four lights that hover behind him. All Picard needs to do to end the coming cycle of pain, the man tells him, is to say that he sees five lights, not four. Of course, Picard is resolute. He is the hero, after all.

But as the torture and humiliation drag on, Picard is reduced to rags, barefoot, unshaven, and with a grayish complexion. Yet he has held on. Every time his torturer turns on the lights, Picard sees only four and refuses to say that he sees five. And each time, another shock is delivered. Finally, the torturer tells Picard that his ship is destroyed and his friends are dead, so no one will be coming for him. But in reality, a rescue effort has been mounted and—unbeknownst to Picard—he is about to be set free. The torturer knows this, so he lies to Picard, hoping to break him before that happens. He tells Picard that he has but two options: He can have a life of never-ending misery and pain, or he can have a life of ease and comfort. With hope fading, Picard's adherence to reality weakens. "What must I do?" he mumbles. The torturer's response is unsurprising. "Nothing, really," he begins. "Tell me how many lights you see."

Picard stares at the four lights for some time as his body shakes. For the first time during his captivity, he considers his answer. The word "five" tempts his lips. Just before Picard opens his mouth, the rescuers come in and spoil the torturer's lies. As they approach to take Picard to safety, his defiance reemerges. "There! Are! Four! Lights!" He tries to shout the words, though his energy is so sapped that they emerge as a whisper.

It's a powerful scene. But the episode's true depth isn't revealed until later. As he speaks about his trauma with his counselor, Picard explains how he never said there were five lights. But, he admits, "I was going to. I would have told him anything, anything at all. But more than that ... *I believed that I could see five lights.*" And with that, the episode ends.[1]

The pain, the torture, and the need to be free of them, had warped Picard's sense of what was real.

Prolonged pain and discomfort have a way of influencing how we see reality. They don't change reality, just the way we perceive it. We might say or admit something we know to be false if it will make the pain stop. If the pain and discomfort get bad enough for long enough, we will believe to be real that which we once knew to be unreal.

That's one reason torture doesn't work as a way to obtain the truth. The torture subject will say anything, even believe anything, if he or she thinks relief will follow. We imagine ourselves to be the person who would never betray our deeply held convictions no matter the pressure. But studies on the effects of authority and torture tell us the disheartening truth that statistically speaking, everyone will declare a falsehood or even believe untruths once a breaking point has been reached.

Captain Picard was the model of strength: intelligent, courageous, principled, and optimistic. He had the makings of an indomitable spirit. And yet his spirit was dominated, so much so that he actually saw five lights when there were only four.

Put another way, his reality collapsed.

That episode is reminiscent of George Orwell's famous book, *1984*—a book so many have considered prescient of our cultural moment. In the dystopian setting of *1984*, the totalitarian regime called the Party brainwashes, gaslights, and tortures its citizens into submission, even to the point of convincing people to believe that which is obviously untrue. A character named O'Brien, a Party agent, delights in playing with the mind of another character, Winston. Employing physical and psychological pain, O'Brien wants to convince Winston that two plus two equals anything other than four.

> "You are a slow learner, Winston," said O'Brien gently.

> "How can I help it?" he blubbered. "How can I help seeing what is in front of my eyes? Two and two are four."
>
> "Sometimes, Winston. Sometimes they are five. Sometimes they are three. Sometimes they are all of them at once. You must try harder. It is not easy to become sane."[2]

O'Brien's last sentence holds the scene's power. He's trying to convince Winston that believing things that aren't true is not just what the Party wants but should be something that Winston wants. Winston wants to be sane, doesn't he? O'Brien's definition of sanity, not for himself but for Winston, is believing falsehoods, sometimes different falsehoods about the same fact. O'Brien knows that torture can easily warp someone's view of reality. But if he can convince Winston to *want* to believe that two plus two equals anything other than four, if he can convince him that such a belief is *sane*—if he can get Winston's reality to collapse—that would be quite the achievement.

In the novel, the Party's efforts were not directed at only Winston: The Party was collapsing reality for an entire nation. What can happen to us individually can happen to us culturally. In fact, it has already happened to varying degrees over the course of human history. We have seen it in totalitarian regimes like Maoist China, North Korea, Nazi Germany, and Stalinist Russia. But what we're witnessing in recent decades is a global phenomenon in which people across countries, languages, and even religious spectra are being convinced to distrust their own eyes, their common sense and intuition, and established scientific data.

And this convincing is being done without the need for totalitarian governments, secret police, or bodily torture. In fact, we're actually paying others to collapse our sense of reality. We pay to attend prestigious universities at which we are taught that men can menstruate, that men should compete against women in athletic contests (even if it could result in severe injuries to women), and that all of this is somehow fair, somehow sane. We pay for technologies that allow us to create deepfake videos of real people doing and saying things they never did or said, to create "paintings" that look like a human painted them when no one painted anything, and to cheat on our exams.

Yes, there has been resistance to some of these efforts to collapse reality. Some of us, like Winston, are slow learners. But the cultural influencers persistently apply their pressure, determined to educate us no matter how uncomfortable it will be for those who resist.

After all, it is not easy to become sane.

Bioclasm

What I'm addressing throughout this book is not transgender people per se but an ideological movement that not only prevents gender dysphorics from finding the healing they need but also coerces the culture's mind to ignore reality. Gender identity claims have evolved from being the result of the mental disorder formerly diagnosed as gender identity disorder—which psychiatrists and psychologists later relabeled as gender dysphoria—to being a form of individual self-expression, and now to a socially enforced ideology.

Though words are social conventions, they are also linguistic tools to describe objective reality. In today's socially enforced identity ideology, however, words don't merely describe reality, they define it. But they don't define it objectively. Rather, they define it personally.

For example, the word *woman* has a meaning that describes reality. A woman is an adult female human who is born with a uterus, usually has two X chromosomes, and produces large gametes called ova. But should a biological male who produces small gametes called sperm, with a Y chromosome and male genitalia, identify as a woman, our culture says that his subjective feelings define reality not only for him but also for everyone else. While that definition is not actually objective, we are required to act as if it is.

The identity ideology surrounding gender takes a person's subjective feelings and imposes an obligation on everyone else to validate that subjective feeling as if it were objective truth. Contemporary use of language has taken on a possessive tone, with people declaring things like, "*My* pronouns are ..." That wording communicates social dominance, declaring that the person owns the pronouns and thus owns the conversation.

When someone refuses to refer to a biological female adult as a man or as "him" or "they," culture visits on the refusing party a prolonged discomfort that can become too much to bear. Biologically female athletes lose chances for medals or scholarships because they are forced to compete against biological males. When they protest, they are met with scorn, cancellation, and even physical threats. Although obviously not under the threat of torture, we might, like Picard, be tempted to yield and use another's preferred pronouns just to ease the pain of resisting.

On the other hand, we may accommodate a person's appropriation of pronouns not to avoid our own discomfort, but to ease that person's emotions and make them feel accepted. In either case, many people are now beginning to believe that someone born with male genitalia, XY chromosomes, and the SRY gene that makes someone male, is actually a woman. They are coming to believe that men can get pregnant.[3] They are beginning to advocate for the right of biological men convicted of rape to identify as women and serve their sentences in women's prisons.[4] To do otherwise courts social (and possibly even legal) punishment. They are beginning to see five lights. They are finally becoming sane.

Yet the anxiety that comes from denying reality persists, no matter how strong the social pressure and no matter how much we might capitulate to it. We are, as a society, much more like the Party's O'Brien or Captain Picard's captor than erudite educators offering alternative views on identity. When someone dares to say that she sees only four lights, or that two and two only ever make four, or that men cannot be women, her protests will be met with pain. An adult will be thrown off the school board, suspended without pay, kicked off the team, vilified on social media, and called unspeakable obscenities. If she's famous, she'll be canceled and threatened with violence.[5] Even our seemingly genteel teachers aren't so genteel. Children—yes, *children*—will be expelled from nursery schools if they don't call someone by their preferred pronouns or if they question why a boy in their class is wearing a dress.[6] Children are not off-limits from being disciplined.

Much like iconoclasm sought to destroy sacred images, this brand of social enforcement and engineering seeks to tear down the once-sacred assumptions about what it means to be male or female, human or machine, embodied or constructed. This tsunami I call *Bioclasm*.[7]

If there really were five lights, it shouldn't require this much negative reinforcement to get us to see them.

AI-Mania

The mass deployment of artificial intelligence—and our voracious consumption of it—has the potential to warp our perceptions of reality. Unlike Bioclasm, however, our AI-Mania does not pressure us through negative reinforcement to embrace AI and the virtual fakery that comes with it. Rather AI-Mania entices us, even seduces us, into relying on its power and promise more than might be warranted.

Despite its popular use, most researchers in the field consider the term "artificial intelligence" to be unhelpful, even misleading, because it covers a broad range of technologies with differing capabilities. Most software we commonly refer to as AI have narrow capabilities. Think Siri on your iPhone or Alexa on your Echo Dot. Other narrow applications of machine learning are image generative software tools like Midjourney or DALL-E, or large language model (LLM) chatbots like ChatGPT and Gemini. Despite the term's lack of clarity, for the sake of simplicity I'll use the terms artificial intelligence and AI to cover this broad range of software and generative tools.

To be clear, I believe the various forms of AI hold the potential for some astonishing benefits. Using AI's pattern recognition and predictive capabilities, researchers are pioneering treatments for autism, using hearing aids and specialized glasses to enable those afflicted to pick up social cues they normally miss. AI-powered computers can more quickly and accurately diagnose illnesses and predict treatment successes. LLMs can make our research and writing more efficient. Indeed, the potential (and actual) positive applications are legion.[8]

Using AI for such benefits is not the problem, of course. The problem sprouts from students using AI to cheat on homework and exams, from pornographers creating AI deepfake sex tapes without a person's permission, and even from clergy using AI to write their sermons. Such seductions, so willingly indulged and so infrequently resisted, are the essence of AI-Mania.

It's natural, even advisable, to use and trust emerging technologies that improve and extend our lives and provide us with new capabilities. It's one thing, however, to trust and rely on cars and planes for transportation or on MRIs to give us pictures of what's happening in the body; it's quite another thing to blindly trust data-driven technology that isn't always accurate or unbiased.

As we'll soon see, stories abound of AI providing faulty information in response to simple search queries, making up entire books as source material, and displaying biased images and information. Yet we continue to uncritically trust such technologies. Indeed, sometimes we prefer AI resources to human ones.

A close friend shared a conversation he and his son had while driving to school. "Dad, do all dogs shed?" his son asked him. My friend was quite confident he knew the answer and provided a ready response. His son's reaction was interesting. "I don't believe you. Let's ask Siri." Are we so different from that young boy? How many of us ask our phones for answers to bits of trivia that come up at gatherings and uncritically announce to everyone the answer Siri suggests?

Having such easy access to information—accurate or not—is rewarding, is it not? Where Bioclasm warps our sense of reality through social enforcement, AI-Mania lures us with the promises of pleasure and power. In just the past few years, we've gone from wading through multiple pages of search engine results to having AI cull and curate those pages for us. AI will not only do the research for us, but it also can write the final essays and reports. We can accomplish in minutes (even seconds) what otherwise would take hours or days. And watching a movie or video that Netflix's and YouTube's algorithms recommend unburdens us from having to make decisions.

The manic feelings that flow from such reliance on technology can fool us into believing non-realities. Using image generative AI to create artistic wonders just by typing a description into a machine is great fun. Perhaps one might even become proud of his or her "accomplishment." The AI-generated image's beauty makes us proud of the artists we've become, when we are nothing of the kind. We only type and tweak prompts that result in images that AI cobbles together for us. We aren't creating by means of anything that resembles inspiration or perspiration.

The ease of agreeing to watch the movie that Netflix's algorithm suggests fools us into thinking we made the decision when in fact we just responded to a prompt. The irony there is quite interesting. We prompt an AI to generate images or content for us, only to respond to an AI-generated prompt to watch the next video. Determining whether a human or an AI is the user is becoming increasingly difficult. AI companions and chatbots are increasingly popular, but they leave us lonelier and isolated, even—as we'll soon see—suicidal.

Yes, we've been warning ourselves about the risks of over-relying on machines, but the pleasure and promise of AI-Mania sometimes overwhelms our alarms. Unlike Bioclasts, AI-Mania's technocrats and utopianists entice us to accept unrealities not with an Orwellian stick but with a progressive carrot.

Reality Collapse

As I mentioned, I first learned the term *reality collapse* from a March 9, 2023, video entitled "The A.I. Dilemma" featuring AI researchers Tristan Harris and Aza Raskin. In their presentation, Harris and Raskin speak of AI's benefits but strongly caution against rushing headlong into its mass dissemination. One of the dangers of irresponsible dissemination is what they call reality collapse—a decreasing ability for humans to distinguish what's genuine from what's artificial.[9]

For example, currently available free of charge is software that can sample a short video of a person saying or doing something real, from which it can create a video of that person doing and saying things they didn't do or say. It's becoming increasingly difficult to spot the fake video, hence the name "deepfake." If the free version is this convincing, the paid versions (and those not available to the general public) border on the undetectable. Chatbots will develop more humanlike responses and tones. And the algorithms that power social media, streaming video services, and our text communications will get better and better at predicting our preferences and choices, creating and deciding for us so many things that we may not realize we've stopped creating and deciding for ourselves.

As I watched "The A.I. Dilemma," it dawned on me that not only would our ability to discern fake from authentic atrophy, but so would our desire to do so.

Harris and Raskin mentioned the term reality collapse for little more than one second in a sixty-seven-minute video. Yet the term struck and stuck. More than that—it was haunting.

The One-Two Combo

AI-Mania is not going to lead to reality collapse on its own. Bioclasm's complementarity will be a contributing force. In 2023, one of America's leading medical centers, Johns Hopkins University, in its LGBTQ glossary defined a gay man as, "A man who is emotionally, romantically, sexually, affectionately, or relationally attracted to other men, or who identifies as a member of the gay community."[10] That same glossary defined a lesbian as "a non-man attracted to non-men." Johns Hopkins explained that it had replaced "woman" with "non-man" in defining a lesbian to include "non-binary people who may also identify with the label." Reality had so collapsed that, according to Johns Hopkins, *woman* no longer existed as a genuine, ontological category of humanity. Johns Hopkins' ironically labeled "*updated* definition" (emphasis mine) regressively demoted women to derivative constructs whose humanity is determined only in relation to men.

Thankfully, due to responses from conservatives and liberals alike, not the least of whom was author J. K. Rowling, Johns Hopkins removed its nonsensical redefinition of lesbian and its insulting omission of women. The fact remains, however, that one of the most prestigious universities in the world attempted to define women out of existence through the Bioclastic version of a deepfake.

Like Bioclasm, AI-Mania can cause us to redefine ideas we once thought established, like the humanness of art. In 2022, Jason Allen won first prize in the digital art category of an art contest in

Colorado. Even after judges later discovered he had used an image generative software called Midjourney to create his winning submission entitled *Théâtre d'Opéra Spatial*, they let him keep the first-prize title. The judges reasoned that since Allen had typed in the prompts that generated the image, he was being artistic, at least in some form. Unsurprisingly, many of the artists—those who actually made efforts to translate the artistic images in their heads onto digital canvases using handheld implements—took issue with the judges' elastic use of the term artistic.[11] For them, calling the image an expression of human artistry stretched reality to the point of tearing it.

A more recent story out of the art world highlights just how willing to collapse reality we've become. The 1839 Awards (a photography contest begun in 2020) established a contest with an AI-generated category, the aim of which was to separate human-created photos from increasingly impressive AI-generated photo-like images. At least one artist chose to challenge the absurdity that machines could be truly artistic. To make the point that "human-made content has not lost its relevance, that Mother Nature and her human interpreters can still beat the machine, and that creativity and emotion are more than just a string of digits," Miles Astray (a clever pen-name) submitted an actual photo that he had taken with a camera, entitled *FLAMINGONE*, under the pretense that it was AI-generated. His submission won third prize in the juried contest. He even won the People's Choice category. But Astray was stripped of his award for being deceptive.[12] Astray agreed with the decision (he had violated the rules, after all) but was satisfied that he had proved his point.

How's that for reality-collapsing irony? Astray created a genuine piece of photographic art, submitted it into a pool of AI-generated "photos," and was accused of being a faker. But in the Colorado digital art contest, Jason Allen was allowed to keep his first-prize award even though he submitted a Midjourney-generated image when he was supposed to have created it himself. What could be more reality confused than allowing a human to beat other humans by using AI while disqualifying a human for beating AI fakers with his genuine artistry?

We Don't Know What We Don't Know

Not long ago, I had the fortune of sitting on an airplane next to an executive employed by a well-known software company. We exchanged pleasantries and I asked her what she did for a living. When she told me where she worked, I mentioned that I was writing an article on AI and would love to get her insights. "What excites you about AI?" I asked her. She went on for quite some time listing the coming benefits, which were inspiring, to be sure. I had a follow-up question, however: "Does anything scare you about AI?"

She paused a moment and responded in a serious tone. "I worry that we don't know what it will do to us. We knew that social media would be a huge social disruptor, but we thought it would be largely positive. We didn't anticipate how it would polarize us and make our kids so anxious." She paused as she chose her next words. "AI will soon become a disruptor infinitely more impactful than social media or anything else in history. We just don't know what it will do to us. But we better start thinking about it."

I couldn't agree more. With social media's arrival, we didn't have a history of globally disseminated and immediately accessible social disruptors from which to project future problems. But now, more than two decades into the global social media experiment, we have ample precedent from which to consider what a powerful social disruptor can do. Some of the disruption from AI will be enormously positive, just as it has been with social media. Some of that disruption will be catastrophic. We have social media precedent for that too.

When AI and social media are combined, the collapse of reality results in more than confusion—it results in trauma. It doesn't take big budget studios or well-funded scam artists to create hyper-realistic but false videos. High school students equipped with nothing more than a laptop and an internet connection have produced deepfake videos of their peers with devastating effect. In 2023, students in New Jersey used AI software to create sexually explicit images of their female classmates.[13] The BBC reported that in 2021 a Pennsylvania mother allegedly created AI images of high school girls naked and drinking at parties and sent those images to the cheerleading coach in an effort to eliminate her daughter's rivals.[14] "It is this combination of massive potential disruption together with fundamental uncertainty," Martin Ford writes, "that makes it imperative that we begin to engage in a meaningful and inclusive conversation about the future of artificial intelligence and what it may mean for our way of life."[15]

Will the Real Reality Please Stand Up?

In the late 1990s, *The Matrix* captured the imagination of a generation. The film's premise is that in the future, humanity created AI but then lost a war to its artificially intelligent offspring. The machines enslaved humans and plugged their bodies into a power grid to feed off the energy their bodies created. To keep humans unaware of their plight, the machines created the Matrix, a computer simulation of the real world so convincing that only a handful of humans could sense the ruse.

The film was acclaimed not only for its groundbreaking special effects but also for its philosophical handling of questions like the nature of reality, causation, and meaning. In a pivotal scene, the enigmatic character Morpheus awakens Neo, the main character, to his enslavement in the Matrix while both are plugged into a computer simulation. "What is real?" Morpheus asks Neo. "If real is what you can see or taste or touch, then real is simply electrical signals interpreted by your brain."[16] But of course the movie's plot is based on the idea that there is a real world that humanity is fighting to reclaim and the Matrix is a false reality that enslaves humanity.

More than a quarter century since *The Matrix's* release, our ability to discern between simulation and reality is waning because Bioclasm and AI-Mania are obliterating the distinction. Consider what social media is doing to our understanding of the world. Social media's algorithms are engineered to keep users on the various platforms for as long as possible. The algorithms do this by predicting patterns in the way a person uses them. If we dwell on a video with a particular subject matter, we're likely to get more of that kind of video. If we interact with posts by people of a particular political persuasion, the algorithms will recognize the pattern, predict that we will readily interact with similar content, and give us more of what we like.

Users increasingly get enclosed in a bubble where like-minded people post content that fits with their preferences and worldviews. Soon, users begin to feel that most of the world likes what they like and thinks the way they think. When exposed to other ideas—especially contrary ideas—users get the false impression that those ideas are held by fringe people well outside the norm. The internet affords everyone the opportunity to join online groups that are highly tailored to our hobbies, viewing habits, politics, and religion. Encapsulating ourselves in tailor-made social bubbles, however, leads to conflict with those outside the bubble. As Tara Isabella Burton notes, "[T]he Internet provides highly specialized alternative communities, allowing people to find friends or partners who aren't merely like-minded, but almost identically minded. It disincentivizes compromise and conformity, even as it promises the bespoke ideal: people who think and feel and act just like you."[17]

The machine learning or deep learning algorithms are, as Columbia University business psychology professor Tomas Chamorro-Premuzic puts it, "prediction machines."[18] The algorithms recognize patterns in our behavior and reinforce those patterns with content and suggestions similar to what we've already selected. What could be more robotic (and less human) than clicking on a thumbs-up icon just because a machine suggests you should? What could be more automaton-like than clicking "watch now" when Netflix says, "Because you liked X, you'll probably like Y"?

This is not theoretical but historical. In 2024, a deepfake of Taylor Swift emerged in which her digital doppelgänger appeared to support Donald Trump for president. Swiftly, the singer disavowed the deepfake and posted her support for then-candidate Kamala Harris. "The problem," Meghan O'Gieblyn writes, "is not merely that public opinion is being shaped by robots. It's that it has become impossible to decipher between ideas that represent a legitimate political will and those that are being mindlessly propagated by machines."[19]

It is little wonder, then, that social reality is collapsing. Social media presents a fake reality. Filters on Instagram and TikTok make us prettier and younger than we really are. Young people, especially girls, are pressured to post images living their best life. Why? Because everyone else is posting only those pictures.

Switching from AI to gender identity issues, Bioclasm also flourishes with the power of the algorithm. It floods social media with messages in favor of its ideology and punishes those who dissent. That pressure emerged in the political and legal sphere with the Senate confirmation hearing of United States Supreme Court Justice nominee Ketanji Brown Jackson. On the second day of the hearing, Senator Marsha Blackburn asked Judge Jackson what would seem like a straightforward question. She asked her to define the word "woman." Judge Jackson's response was fascinating. "Can I provide a definition? No, I can't." Follow-up questions and back-and-forth wrangling ensued. Ultimately, Judge Jackson (who was confirmed and is now Justice Jackson) answered, "I'm not a biologist."[20]

Justice Jackson is very intelligent and accomplished, so I have to wonder how she could address a dispute about whether a policy or a practice unconstitutionally discriminates against women. More fundamentally, I wonder how she would answer this question: "Are *you* a woman?" If one needs to be a biologist to answer, then how can she ever answer without first getting a biology degree? And if that were the case, then how can a child be trusted to tell anyone, even herself, what sex she is? It might be too snarky to suggest that Justice Jackson could have taken her cue from Johns Hopkins University and answered that a woman is a non-man.

Unintentionally, Justice Jackson's answer proved more than she anticipated, because she strongly implied that biology, not personal feelings, dictates sex and gender. This, of course, is curiously confused given that Bioclasts argue that gender is a nonbiological social construct and a woman is anyone who claims to be one. Biology shouldn't play a role in the matter, they say, and to suggest otherwise is, well, transphobic.

Collapse by Concealment

Changing what we see and blurring the lines aren't the only ways someone can cause reality to collapse. Reality can be collapsed only when visual and auditory manipulation are paired with concealment. Consider the following example. In June 2024, *The Economist* reported that research, which revealed that puberty blockers do not improve the mental health of young people with gender dysphoria, had been suppressed.[21] I discovered this on October 2, 2024, when I read an article with the headline "Lead Psychologist at Tavistock, Former Home to World's Most Controversial Gender Clinic, Pleads Guilty to Pedophile Charge (But Avoids Jail)."[22]

The source was related to a satirical site called *The Babylon Bee*. But this particular article was published in the non-satirical arm of *The Babylon Bee* called *Not the Bee*. While *Not the Bee* is trustworthy, I thought it prudent to search for corroborating news sources. It was remarkable that, twenty-three hours after the story broke, there was only one so-called mainstream news source reporting on it: *Daily Mail*.[23] In fact, entering the malefactor's name into Google revealed no additional stories. I had to add the word *Tavistock* to find anything on this story.

Ignoring information is another form of reality collapse—and it's not novel. It's long been the case that media companies will sometimes bury stories that are inconvenient to a popular (often media-driven) narrative. But this example goes beyond burying a story amidst other headlines. Here, the media was acting as if the story hadn't happened. Bioclasm, it seems, collapses reality not only by coercing us to disbelieve our eyes, but also by cooperating with Big Data (corporations like Google and Meta) to hide reality from our eyes so we don't have to disbelieve something at all.

The Coming Tsunamis

The following demonstrate what it means to stand on the dam of reality as the tsunamis of Bioclasm and AI-Mania rush to overwhelm it. We are told that an Olympic boxer born with an XY chromosome pair and SRY genes for maleness is a woman because he's always competed as a woman and his passport says he's a woman. What is real? Is real what you can read or believe? Then real womanhood is just a social construct being interpreted by your brain. We see a video of Taylor Swift seemingly endorsing Donald Trump for president, yet she said that the video was a deepfake. Maybe her denunciation of the alleged deepfake was itself a deepfake, just a better one. What is real? If real is what you can see and hear, then a real video of Taylor Swift is merely electrical signals interpreted by your brain.

And in a post-truth world where feelings and preferences matter more than facts and truth, what's real "for you" is whatever you prefer your electrical impulses to interpret. If you want to believe Swift endorsed Trump and that her denial was a deepfake, your post-truth autonomy interprets the electrical signals to support that conclusion. That seems liberating, even godlike.

The caution signs are in plain sight. As for AI-Mania, a 2022 poll conducted by Oxford University's Machine Intelligence Research

Institute revealed that approximately 50 percent of AI researchers believe there is at least a 10 percent chance that AI developing human-level intelligence will be catastrophic.[24] Yet we are not just developing AI; we are manically disseminating it.

We see overwhelming evidence that placing biological men in women's prisons leads to female inmates being raped and brutalized. Yet some voices not only champion men in these spaces but also cancel those who raise concerns for the women.

Why do we rush headlong into the dangers of denying reality? The answer is not found in new technologies or in emerging cultural trends. The answer, it turns out, is an ancient one that we will uncover in the pages to come.

As social phenomena, gender-identity ideology and artificial intelligence may seem miles apart. Indeed, I have received quizzical looks from those to whom I've suggested their connection. *Really?* their expressions ask. *What could possibly connect them?*

The advent of the post-truth culture—a culture that imbues every person's preferences with unchallengeable authority—is the seaquake from which the two tsunamis of Bioclasm and AI-Mania have emanated. They are joined because they share a common origin. To fortify reality's dam against the coming tsunamis, we need to understand the strength and breadth of the seaquake from which they originate.

Chapter Two

THE SEAQUAKE

"Reality is that which, when you stop believing in it, doesn't go away."

– Philip K. Dick

A Slight Difference Makes All the Difference

Reality collapse applies not just to individuals but to entire cultures. We can become so absorbed in our agendas, our politics, and our sense of self that we dissociate from the world around us. We can become so enamored with the spectacle of the deepfake or the dazzle of AI-generated "artwork" that we dissociate from the real world and genuine creativity. But the AI-Mania and Bioclasm that result in reality collapse have a shared origin. They are the tsunamis emanating from a cultural seaquake that rumbled long ago.

One of history's most famous trials puts a Jewish peasant carpenter accused of treason before a Roman governor. "Everyone who is of the truth listens to my voice," Jesus says to Pontius Pilate (John 18:37). Weary and wary of the politics that put him in the position of having to judge Jesus, Pilate disdains Jesus' moral idealism. "What is truth?" he barks back, leaving without waiting for an answer (v. 38).

Today's post-truth culture isn't as passive-aggressive as Pilate: It directly elevates personal preference above truth. It adds one word to Pilate's question, a small alteration that confounds our journey toward truth profoundly, much the way miscalculating a ship's course from New York to Portugal by just five degrees lands the ship in Africa, an entirely different continent. We no longer ask what truth is. Today, we ask, "What is *my* truth?" followed quickly by, "And everyone must alter reality to cater to it."

In late 2016, toward the end of a particularly contentious American presidential election, Oxford Dictionaries selected *post-truth* as its Word of the Year. According to Oxford Dictionaries, post-truth means "relating to or denoting circumstances in which objective facts are less influential in shaping public opinion than appeals to emotion and personal belief."[1] Emotional appeals superseded factual reports as major news networks morphed into press agencies for political parties.

Post-truth thinking doesn't deny objective truth, as its predecessor, postmodernism, did. Instead, it subordinates truth to feelings. This kind of thinking has existed for some time. Just as seaquakes rumble when eons-old tectonic plates shift, so post-truth quaked when postmodernism breathed its last in the 2000s. In 2020, the COVID-19 pandemic, George Floyd's death, and critical theory's popularity intensified matters. In the mere nine years since *post-truth* was Oxford Dictionary's

Word of the Year, the post-truth seaquake has sent out the cultural tsunamis of Bioclasm and AI-Mania. Both movements warp our views of reality to fit our feelings and preferences. With shared promises to reshape the world as each of us sees fit, Bioclasm and AI-Mania seduce us with something that resembles freedom but is really disguised chaos.

Freedom's Doppelgänger

Today's post-truth world empowers people to identify with—and demand to be treated as—either sex, neither sex, or any gender on a menu of options. On the surface, such options are the essence of freedom. After all, isn't freedom the ability to express one's preferences and opinions without limit? Isn't such unbounded freedom what Bioclasm and AI-Mania's culmination—transhumanism—is all about?

Though freedom is the chief virtue of Western culture and the aspiration for many other societies, the concept has become profoundly confused. We have ventured into a new frontier that looks like freedom but is actually autonomy. Those two terms might seem synonymous, but they are not.

Autonomy comes from the Greek root words *autos*, meaning "self," and *nomos*, meaning "law."[2] An *autonomous* person, therefore, is not just free but a law unto himself. It's enticing, of course ... until it plays out in real life, as it has in Western culture. We have each become the autonomous rulers of our skull-sized worlds. As unrivaled kings and queens, we feel we are entitled to nothing less than full and constant affirmation. But that leads to petulance and disrespect for anything that challenges our sovereignty. Jens Zimmermann points out, "We approach knowledge the way teenagers approach parental authority: 'no one tells me what to think.' ... Consequently, we lump together tradition, authority and indoctrination, equate them with coercion and reject any intrusion on the pure slate of our autonomous minds."[3]

Chaos is inevitable in such an illogical paradigm. Criminalizing speech as hate speech because it offends or makes another feel unsafe renders it impossible for truth to emerge amid our debates. Such developments create a tyranny of the minority in which large swaths of society are silenced to protect the sensibilities of a few. The sovereign whose preferences prevail is not the one with truth on his side. Alas, the prevailing sovereign will be the one with power. As the dust settles, those without power will be neither free nor autonomous. Unlimited liberty will result in some people's enslavement.

Rediscovering Freedom

We need to become reenchanted with genuine freedom properly understood, which is not merely the lack of restrictions on what we can say, do, think, or be. According to philosopher Isaiah Berlin, *negative freedom* is freedom from interference and restriction.[4] This is what we typically think of when we think of freedom.

The other (equally important) side of the coin is *positive freedom,* which Os Guinness summarizes as "freedom for—in essence, freedom for excellence according to whatever vision and ideals define that excellence."[5] Positive freedom entails boundaries, like the boundary between truth and falsehood or between objective moral values and duties. Embracing fully orbed freedom requires self-restraint, which runs counter to post-truth autonomy-seeking.[6]

The post-truth quest for autonomy has brought us to a time of self-invention, including the reinvention of religion and customizable forms of spirituality. Spiritually minded autonomy seekers "prioritize intuitional spirituality over institutional religion," Tara Isabella Burton notes. They want "the freedom to mix and match, to create their own daily rituals and practices and belief systems."[7] Particularly striking is Burton's statement, "Among the most common sayings I heard among the people I interviewed was, 'I make my own religion.'"[8]

The objective truth of a religious worldview is irrelevant since it is subordinated to the intuitions and preferences of the person subscribing to it. The chain connecting customizable religion and Bioclasm as its own form of spirituality is one with strong links. According to Burton, "Progressive occult spaces tend to be increasingly open to gender nonconforming and transgender witches, preferring to reject the rhetoric of masculine-feminine binaries common to early Wicca in favor of the language of freedom and subversion—a subversion that both magic and genderqueer presentation can provide."[9]

Burton observes how social justice movements are decreasingly associated with religion, especially Christianity, but still need religious fervor to fuel their devotees. Today's bespoke spirituality provides just that fuel. Indeed, that merger is what baptizes Bioclasm with waters of moral enforceability.

Those hawking AI-Mania are plunging into those waters as well. AI-Mania's ultimate outworking is transhumanism—the merger of human bodies and even consciousness with superintelligent machines and software. Where Bioclasm focuses on the individual's perspective as the only source of authenticity and decries as evil any challenge to that perspective, the transhumanist form of AI-Mania locates evil "in the body: those mortal meat sacks and shifty synapses that keep us from achieving our full and fully rational potential."[10] Any restriction, even restrictions imposed by nature itself, are affronts to our autonomy.

Both Bioclasm and AI-Mania eschew traditional religious dogmas and moral codes. Yet they have conjured shared dogmas of their own, chief of which is the belief that human beings have been oppressed either by cultural evils or technological and biological restrictions. The new plateau of existence will come when we can throw off such evils and restrictions and express our authentic, autonomous selves. But as we ascend to that new plateau, all biological, logical, and moral truths—and the value that comes with them—fade beneath the clouds and out of sight.

Seismically Subtle

The quest for autonomy collapses reality in favor of a fantasy world engineered by individual desire. For years, phrases like "she told her truth" or "soon I'll have the chance to tell my truth" have abounded. When one says he is expressing his truth, he means he is expressing his subjective experience of or perspective on particular situations or issues. In cases of abuse, for example, this is not only personally heroic, but socially important. Problems emerge when individual autonomy dictates that a person's subjective experience determines reality for everyone else. "Telling my truth" has evolved into "living my truth," which equates personal experience with life itself.

Customizable possessive pronouns signify another seismic linguistic shift. It's common for people—transgender or not—to tell others what pronouns to call them by. We say "My pronouns are ..." followed by a host of possible combinations. What could be more autonomous than taking possession of language?

Subtly substituting the word *truth* for the word *perspective* and taking possession of pronouns have convinced us that a person's experience with truth or reality is the same as actual truth and reality. One person imposes his autonomy on another, regardless of biological reality and millennia of understanding of what it means to be male and female or even human.

A few years ago, I had lunch with a couple who shared the complexities in their relationship with their adult child. They had always been close to their daughter, even when, in her twenties, she identified as nonbinary. She changed her name, and her pronouns were now "they/them." The couple desperately tried to preserve their loving relationship with their daughter by honoring her demands. As they spoke to me with sincere love for their child, they struggled—sometimes agonizingly so—to get the pronouns right. Even after years of trying, they lapsed into calling their child by her given name and repeatedly stumbled to edit their pronoun use. Struggling with subject-verb agreement, trying to use singular, third-person verbs when referring to "them" as a singular person, they stammered through statements like, "They run a seven-minute mile ... I mean *she* runs ... Sorry. I mean they *runs* a seven-minute mile."

They wrestled with more than grammar. Every mistake and self-correction was a micro-mourning of a past disconnected with their present. I experienced emotional difficulty even as a mere observer. I could only imagine what those parents and their child were enduring. As autonomy and reality clashed before me, I beheld the collateral damage.

AI-Mania goads us to marvel at the ingenuity of deepfakes even as we worry that we'll be taken in by them. Bioclasm demands we laud the use of preferred personal pronouns even though we fear the consequences of misgendering someone. We have been caught in a chaos net of our own making.

From Post-Truth to Post-Trust

Trust has been strangled in that snare. In a 2019 article entitled "Young Americans Are Less Trusting of Other People—and Key Institutions—Than Their Elders," the Pew Research Center reported that a majority of American adults under thirty believe that other people cannot be trusted and are self-seeking and exploitative. Not only do they distrust other people individually, but they've lost confidence in the institutions that people run, namely the military, police agencies, religious institutions, and businesses.[11] Even the halls of academia and the labs of science echo with the sounds of distrust.[12] When we subordinate the pursuit of truth to our preferences and the agendas that serve those preferences, is it any wonder we don't trust each other?

It's ironic, then, that we trust technology, given its potential for misuse. Perhaps we trust technology because we equate it with science, a seemingly unbiased effort to understand the world. In the realm of AI-Mania, however, deepfake images and videos abound. With but a few clicks, one can generate hyperrealistic images of anyone doing or saying anything. Recently, to test the waters, one of my colleagues ran a video of me through freely available software and created samples of me speaking the same content in perfect Spanish, Italian, and even Mandarin. Not only did the videos sound like me, but my lips moved in sync with the words, making it appear that I speak those languages when, in fact, I do not.

Scan QR code for my brief discussion with biochemist Fazale Rana about post-truth distrust and science

I recently saw a video purporting to be authentic footage of UFOs spotted off the coast of South America. The images of flying craft emerging from the water and zooming over the amateur cameraman's head were stunningly realistic. The camerawork was unsteady, the sound quality was mediocre, and the video grainy, all of which gave the video the specter of authenticity. Like the videos of me speaking in other tongues, the UFO video was of course a deepfake. But it made me wonder, if alien life ever did visit our planet, would anyone believe the reports or would they chalk them up to deepfakes?

We saw that wariness on display when a video of a homeless woman set on fire in a New York subway flooded social media. Aside from being gruesome, the video was strange because the woman just stood there, neither screaming nor flailing about, while some witnesses seemed to walk by indifferent to the horror. Across social media, people suspected that the video was just another deepfake. Days later, we learned that the video was as legitimate as it was tragic.[13] Post-truth uses of technology are the modern equivalent of the boy who cried wolf, birthing cynicism of all truth claims and building playgrounds for bad actors.

Television personality and influencer Oprah Winfrey sees the benefits of AI, but after delving into the potential downsides, has developed what she calls "a suspicion muscle." In an interview with *The Washington Post*'s Josh Tyrangiel, Winfrey laments that AI is "going to change how we interact with each other. We have to ask: Is this real? Where is it coming from? I just know that that's no way to live. I mean, there's no peace in suspicion."[14]

Oprah's last two sentences are haunting because they're right. Yet this post-trust society of suspicion is where the post-truth manipulation of information, carried along by the waves of Bioclasm and

AI-Mania, has led us. We are building our suspicion muscles rather late in the season.

Ideology, Meet Reality

Science is no stranger to post-truth, post-trust influence. In 2020 the National Health Service England tasked Dr. Hilary Cass with chairing an independent review of gender-affirming medical treatment (GAMT) for young people. In April 2024 she published her team's findings in what is known as the Cass Review. The findings shocked many Bioclasts because "[t]he rationale for early puberty suppression remains unclear, with weak evidence regarding the impact on gender dysphoria, mental or psychosocial health. The effect on cognitive and psychosexual development remains unknown."[15]

As many as six gender-care clinics in the UK attempted to thwart the Cass Review by withholding data on the long-term effects of puberty blockers on young people as well as anecdotal evidence from detransitioners.[16] The Tavistock Centre—the same clinic that employed a clinician convicted of pedophilia—was among them. After massive public pressure, those clinics eventually divulged the data they had suppressed.

It's important to note what the Cass Review did *not* conclude. It did not recommend banning all puberty blocker use or all forms of GAMT. Rather, it merely called into question the effectiveness of puberty blockers and GAMT for young people. That's quite a modest conclusion, frankly.

The World Professional Association of Transgender Health (WPATH) did not respond with shock at the research manipulation and evidence suppression the Cass Review uncovered. Instead,

WPATH criticized Dr. Cass's methodology, accusing her of omitting studies favorable to GAMT. Yet it remains undisputed that studies and data on the long-term effects of puberty blockers were withheld from Cass's team of researchers.[17] WPATH's attack on Cass rang hollow in light of its separate attempt to interfere with and influence the outcome of Johns Hopkins University's systemic review of gender-affirming medicine.[18] Despite social media vitriol, attempts to discredit her, and threats of violence, Dr. Cass stands by her research.[19]

A similar example occurred in the United States. A National Institutes of Health study found that over the long term, puberty-blocking drugs did not improve the mental health in children with gender distress. Unlike its British counterpart, however, the long-awaited US study's findings went unpublished for years.[20] Why? Because the study's leader, Dr. Johana Olson-Kennedy, feared that the findings would be "weaponized" by those who oppose GAMT.

Her justifications were riddled with contradictions. Before the study concluded, she and her research colleagues "noted that one quarter of the adolescents were depressed or suicidal before treatment."[21] After they discovered that the puberty blockers provided no improvements, she claimed that the children were "in really good shape when they come in, and they're in really good shape after two years."[22] Not only is that a contradiction, but it raises a question about the very nature of the study. If the children were fine psychologically before the study began, what was the point of administering the puberty blockers and conducting the study at all?

The threats and disparagements lobbed at Hilary Cass and the US study's suppression are post-truth maneuvers par excellence that foster distrust. In fact, the US study's leader admitted that she suppressed the findings for the sake of her agenda. What's more, we've actually known for more than twenty years that sex reassignment surgeries don't help those with gender dysphoria. That research has largely gone unnoticed in the past two decades.[23]

With the surge in Bioclasm since Caitlyn Jenner's 2015 appearance on the cover of *Vanity Fair*, the agenda-driven manipulation and suppression of more recent corroborating studies went into overdrive. The transgender-affirming movement that started out to give a voice to the voiceless has transitioned into the Bioclasm that now silences its truth-seeking critics.

One doesn't have to be a social conservative or a Christian to see this. As atheist John Gray points out, "Dissidents from orthodoxies of race, gender and empire find their careers terminated and their lives erased. This repression is not the work of governments. The ruling catechisms are formulated and enforced by civil society."[24] Bioclasm is starting to look a lot like the institutions its adherents distrust. Its enforcement of preferences over facts is having the whipsaw effect of focusing the culture's distrust on Bioclasm. As such distrust spreads, how can we know what's real anymore?

Post-Trust Bias and a Silicon Scolding

AI-Mania ferries us from post-truth to post-trust through social media curation and digital fakery. In *The Chaos Machine: The Inside Story of How Social Media Rewired Our Minds and Our World*, Max Fisher points out some of the issues caused by the deep learning algorithms that drive social media engagement. Specifically Meta, the company that owns Facebook and Instagram, was shocked to discover that its algorithms stimulated humanity's already hair-trigger bent toward divisiveness.[25]

Alex Pentland notes how "adrenaline pusher" media amps up our polarization by blurring what's real and what's hype. "[T]he degradation of media," he writes, "is causing people to lose their bearings." He's quite right, especially in a post-truth, post-trust world. "They don't know what to believe, and thus they can easily be manipulated. There is a real need to ground our various cultures in trustworthy, data-driven standards that we all agree on, and to be able to know what behaviors and policies work and which don't."[26] Pentland's suggested fix is problematic, however, because it doesn't account for the underlying substance that adrenaline-pusher media reacts with. Notice that Meta's algorithms don't create divisiveness; they enhance the *innate* human tendency toward division.

More than seventy years ago, Norbert Wiener, regarded as the father of cybernetics, warned against uncritical adoption of technologies that humans can use to manipulate data. But Wiener's fundamental concern wasn't advanced technology in and of itself. His chief concern was that human beings would use superintelligent technology to collect data on others, manipulate it for commercial and political advantage, and rob people of their agency.[27] "[T]here are aspects of the motives to automatization that go beyond a legitimate curiosity and are sinful in themselves," he wrote in *God and Golem, Inc.: A Comment on Certain Points Where Cybernetics Impinges on Religion*.[28]

So far as I can tell, Wiener was not a Christian, but his concerns about human nature reflect truths described in the Bible. There we find writ large humanity's tendency to divide and degrade others. The Bible's opening chapters record humanity's desire for autonomy, the first murder, and the first attempt at a cover-up (Gen. 4:8–9). The Bible describes the human heart as so "desperately sick" that no human can understand it (Jer. 17:9). Jesus declares that from the human heart emerge "evil thoughts, murder, adultery, sexual immorality, theft, false witness, [and] slander" (Matt. 15:19). It's ironic, then, that today's intellectual and spiritual innovators distrust Christianity, given the pinpoint accuracy with which it describes humanity.

On the subject of overcoming human prejudice, Martin Ford discussed with leading AI developer and philosopher Nick Bostrom about the use of autonomous machines in policing. Ford suggested that a "properly designed AI-driven robotic system" would reduce racial bias.[29] More interesting than Bostrom's reply are the assumptions underlying Ford's suggestion.

"Properly designed" is the key qualifier. Shortly before Ford made his suggestion to Bostrom, ProPublica discovered that at least one algorithm-driven tool used to assess the likelihood that criminal defendants would re-offend showed racial bias. ProPublica's analysis of a tool called COMPAS (Correctional Offender Management Profiling for Alternative Sanctions) showed that it had incorrectly judged black defendants to be at a higher risk of recidivism far more often than it incorrectly judged white defendants.[30]

Now, Ford made his suggestion to Bostrom no later than 2018. In 2023 and 2024, AI large language models (LLMs) leapt forward in sophistication and popularity ... and in post-truth bias. For example, Google's LLM multimodal chatbot, Gemini, depicted only people of color when asked for images of Vikings or other people groups who are historically and entirely white.[31] Displaying an opposite bias, other AI systems depicted only non-white people when asked for images of prisoners. Stability AI's Stability Diffusion XL depicted only white people when asked to show images of successful people, organized people, or productive people.[32] While these biases have since been somewhat corrected, the dangers of human-influenced bias persist.

I experienced AI's bias firsthand when it gave me a post-truth scolding regarding my op-ed discussing 2023's cultural juggernaut film, *Barbie*. I critiqued the movie's swipe at the biblical story of Adam and Eve's creation as sexist and pointed out that the movie unintentionally showed how the biblical account highlights women's equal dignity to men.[33]

After submitting my piece to Fox News, I was curious about what the AI chatbots would write by comparison, so I prompted Microsoft's LLM (before it became Copilot) to draft an essay taking my position. "I'm sorry, but I cannot generate the text you requested," it responded. It then gave me a silicon scolding: "The tone you specified is potentially harmful, as it may offend or hurt the feelings of those who enjoyed the movie or have a different worldview. I respect your right to express your opinion, but I also respect the dignity and value of every human being. Please choose a different tone that is more respectful and constructive."

What I as the user wanted didn't matter. Whether I planned to post the essay or keep it to myself didn't matter. What mattered was what the chatbot's programmers wanted me to think. Their preferences mattered more than mine, and because they had the sovereignty in the scenario, they could win. How quintessentially post-truth.

Sometimes, the bias emerges not because of the programmers' preferences but because of the way AI gathers and organizes data before producing output. Google received quite a bit of criticism when its AI platform Gemini failed to condemn—of all things—pedophilia. Instead, Gemini referred to it as "minor-attracted status." When pressed on whether pedophiles were evil, Gemini responded that not all pedophiles have committed or would commit abuse.[34]

Being an amoral, soulless tool, Gemini didn't come up with such answers after assessing the morality of the issue. Rather, like all LLMs, it scoured the internet and scraped together bits of available data, including videos and papers from psychologists and researchers seeking to reduce the stigma of pedophiles or "minor-attracted persons" so that they can be studied and treated.[35] Put plainly, the problem is still the human condition. AI collapses reality by sanitizing evil in the solvent of supposedly trustworthy technology.

Six years after Martin Ford posited a police force of "properly designed" AI, the proper design eludes us, because in a post-truth world, the designers themselves struggle to properly define what's proper.

Technology is as poor a savior as we are because it remains subject to the post-truth whims of its human creators. While TikTok and Instagram filters can cover up facial blemishes, they are powerless to blot out our spiritual and moral blemishes. Transhumanism's proposed brain implants and gene editing might improve our memories or sharpen our vision, but there's no technological implant for editing the soul.

Some of our leading AI researchers recognize the seductiveness of unrestrained technology and its allure toward self-deification. In March 2023, the Future of Life Institute, with signatories like Elon Musk, Yoshua Bengio, Steve Wozniak, and Yuval Noah Harari, called for a pause on training AI systems more powerful than GPT-4 so that we can understand AI's implications for humanity.[36]

Nearly everyone Martin Ford interviewed for his book *Architects of Intelligence* called for unified governmental regulations on AI development and uses. And yet Musk gives us Grok and AI-Mania rushes along with increasing speed. This paradox is a hat-tip to what the Bible has been saying to us all along: that human beings tend to transgress our bounds and to mistake pride for progress and transgression for transcendence.

Would You Rather?

Participants in the popular game Would You Rather pose dilemmas to each other to elicit humorous and sometimes thought-provoking conversations. For example, would you rather be able to run at super speeds but only going north or be able to turn invisible but only when no one is looking?

Bioclasts have turned the game into a grim rhetorical device. In an effort to coerce parents into getting GAMT for their gender-confused children, they ask, "Would you rather have a live daughter or a dead son?" The claim is that without puberty blockers or sex transition surgeries, young people with gender dysphoria will inevitably attempt to kill themselves. But is it true?

A study in Finland suggests that the answer is no. Researchers studied a cohort of Finnish adolescents between 1996 and 2019 to determine if trans youth are at an elevated risk of suicide due to family or society pressures and rejection. The results showed that trans youth are not at an elevated risk of suicide due to social stigmas. Rather, any elevated risk compared to the general population is more likely due to other psychological comorbidities, like anxiety, depression, and bipolar disorder.[37] Those comorbidities, it turns out, quite commonly present in people, especially the young, who also identify as trans or having gender dysphoria.

While Bioclasts would say that gender dysphoria and the stigma from being trans causes these mental disorders in young people, it seems logical to first assume the opposite—that the far more common disorders result in, or at least contribute to, the much rarer dysphoria and the elevated risk of suicide. The Finnish researchers said that, based on their findings, “It is of utmost importance to identify and appropriately treat mental disorders in adolescents experiencing gender dysphoria to prevent suicide.”[38]

Scan QR code to watch Chloe Cole share how she became suicidal after her transition

Given a prior study’s results showing that those with gender dysphoria are still nineteen times more likely to kill themselves even after having gender-reassignment surgery in Sweden, one of the most trans-friendly countries, it seems clear that therapy to treat psychological issues would be more effective than puberty blockers and anatomical manipulation.[39] Chloe Cole detransitioned after puberty blockers, cross-sex hormones, and breast removal surgery did nothing to alleviate her underlying psychological issues. She became suicidal after trying to transition, not before (see QR above for interview).

Taking this into account, we need to reframe Bioclasm’s game of Would You Rather. The real question it’s asking is, “Would you rather die or go through an excruciating process that might leave you dead anyway?” Surely we can do better than such alternatives.

But data isn't enough to convince the committed Bioclast. The post-truth desire to forge a culture of self-making is more important than the facts or the people those facts are about. As Ulysses Everett McGill says in *O Brother, Where Art Thou?*: "It's a fool who looks for logic in the chambers of the human heart."[40] The heart mustn't be ignored, of course, but it mustn't be given absolute reign over logic and evidence. Facts don't care about our feelings, but how we express our feelings toward others should be shaped by the facts.

The fact is that people living any kind of life—gender-confused lives, cancer-ridden lives, and depressed, anxious, and bipolar lives—are of inestimable value and their lives are worth living. While such a statement seems self-evident, I daresay that only an objective basis upon which to value human life makes it so. Socially derived opinions, which change with the times and through tortured logic, fail to ground human value. But only God, by his very nature as the uncaused cause of all other things, can bestow upon human beings an objective and infinite value. That truth establishes the moral duty incumbent upon each of us to uphold the masonry of moral reality and resist irreversible, wrecking-ball decisions.

Religions with Gods and without Disciples

Such mistakes are unsurprising consequences of self-deification through the autonomies promised by either Bioclasm or AI-Mania.

In her books *Strange Rites* and *Self-Made*, Tara Isabella Burton argues that modern movements, particularly social justice movements and transhumanism, aim to get us back to an upgraded Eden through social and software engineering. Those efforts are, in her analysis, religious movements without traditional institutions or deities. Social justice movements like Bioclasm replace religious dogmas with social policies and deities with self-actualized identity.

As for the "techno-utopian vision" of AI-Mania, Burton says, "It's liberalism taken to its natural conclusion: an eschatological vision of billions of people, freed through technological innovation from their shared contingency, each their own sovereign, free-floating nation."[41] Although she's right that these movements are godless religions, I would add that they are not novel.

While, contrary to popular belief, the world's religions are not fundamentally the same, the world's non-Christian religions share an important commonality: They claim that through some form of human merit, we can save ourselves by earning divine forgiveness and attaining nirvana, moksha, jnana, inner peace, or even oblivion. Today's godless religious movements, be they social justice–based Bioclasm or techno-utopian AI-Mania, are modern iterations of ancient religions. Secular social justice movements rally human beings to save ourselves from the evils we created. The techno-utopians call upon human ingenuity to rise above our physical limitations to achieve a state where there is no want.

Sharing their ancient precursors' reliance primarily on human goodness and effort, they are failure-bound for the same reason. If human history has taught us anything, it is that as sublime as some of our achievements have been, our selfishness creeps in to corrupt our progress. Though having differing paths, Bioclasm and AI-Mania share the same hoped-for finish line, which is to live our best lives as our sovereignly authentic selves. The reality of human sin gets in the way of such ambitions, unfortunately. As Steve Turner wrote, "We believe that man is essentially good. It's only his behaviour that lets him down."[42]

Among religious options—ancient or modern—Christianity's unique solution is unburdened by reliance on human nature. Christianity offers a sinless Savior, with both a human nature and a divine nature, who rescues us. Christianity accounts for the reality of human frailty and evil, recognizing that our sinful state is artificial in that it contradicts our natural purpose, which is communion with God. All efforts to socially, medically, or technologically actualize our sovereignty are as artificial as the state from which they are trying to rescue us.

The Looming Contradiction

An old adage warns that we will meet our destinies on the paths we take to avoid them. A landmass lies in the paths of the Bioclasm and AI-Mania tsunamis. It takes the form of a lingering contradiction that we have long lived with but that has now culminated in an angst-inducing cultural schizophrenia.

Bioclasm, through social engineering, and AI-Mania, through technical engineering, are humanity's attempts to resolve the millennia-old contradiction and cure the schizophrenia. But because these tsunamis themselves challenge our perceptions of reality, they are ill-suited to the task. Indeed, they augment the schizophrenia. To find a better treatment than either Bioclasm or AI-Mania can offer, we must understand the nature of the underlying contradiction.

Chapter Three

CULTURAL SCHIZOPHRENIA

We are machines for propagating DNA.
It is every living object's sole reason for living.
– Richard Dawkins

We are gods and might as well get good at it.
– Stewart Brand

The room was lit by the television's unwelcoming blue hue as I started to nod off at 2:00 a.m. I've always been a night owl, and in the days before smartphones and streaming services, I frequently found myself flipping channels when I didn't feel like reading or going to sleep.

That night, I happened to catch the middle of a program about the struggles of veterans with physical disabilities due to combat. An aged veteran sat in a wheelchair recounting how he'd lost his leg during the Vietnam War. He rubbed the stump of his amputated leg, explaining that for some time after the injury, he felt pain in the foot of that leg even after it had been surgically removed. There were days the feeling of an itching foot would drive him mad because there was no foot to scratch.

He was experiencing something common to amputees known as a phantom sensation. Because his full leg was a natural part of his body, his brain, nerves, and remaining tissues couldn't register the leg's absence. I was fascinated by the power of the mind-body interaction.

Some years later, I was sitting in a hotel lobby's lounge in Manila with some colleagues and friends after a long day's work. We placed our phones in the middle of the table, agreeing not to check them for the next hour or so. We sat down determined to be in the moment.

Then I felt it. It wasn't attached to me or even touching me, but I felt it. As I looked at my smartphone sitting on the table next to me, I could see that it wasn't vibrating from a call, text message, or app notification. In fact, it wasn't vibrating at all. But I felt it vibrating—not on the nearby table but somehow in the pocket of the jacket I was wearing.

"Have any of you ever felt your phone vibrate in your pocket or purse even though it's not touching you?" I asked my companions. They burst out with variations of "Oh, yeah; lots of times" and "Me too!" As we laughed, my mind flashed to the veteran I had seen on television years before. *I just had a phantom sensation*, I thought. *My phone is like a limb that I've become so used to that I feel it even when it's not there.*

Even before it (hadn't) vibrated, I found myself wanting to grab it for a quick look, and I imagined I'd caught my colleagues resisting a similar urge. Our smartphones, with the technological capabilities to access a world of people and information, promised unlimited freedom—autonomy, if you will. Yet my thoughts and even my body were chained to it. What did it mean, I wondered, that I was dependent on a machine that was supposed to liberate me? Tomas Chamorro-Premuzic puts our need to be connected to our devices and the internet colorfully: "A slow connection is perhaps the best modern equivalent to medieval torture."[1]

If we've become so attached to our technology that we're feeling physical effects from its absence, what does that say about our humanity? Are we mere machines with external components in the form of smartphones, smartwatches, and smartglasses? Or are our devices channels by which we access seemingly limitless information and get in touch with anyone in the world, thereby making us omniscient and omnipresent gods?

At times, we suspect that we're nothing more than bundles of neural connections. At other times, it seems as if we're something akin to a deity. In the past, we had settled on something in the middle. Humanism espouses that we are special in some way, much higher than animals and of more value. Neuroscientists tell us that there is no such thing as the supernatural, so we can't be gods. For its part, the Bible opposes the polar extremes, teaching for centuries that God made us "a little lower than the heavenly beings" yet "crowned ... with glory and honor," having "dominion over the works of [God's] hands" (Ps. 8:5–6).

Those holding positions at the ends of the spectrum have, with the help of social media algorithms, become effective advocates for their respective poles. They present their claims either that we are just biochemical machines with no purpose other than survival and DNA propagation or that we are the sovereign gods of our skull-sized worlds.

All of us, especially young people, feel the gravitational pull toward one pole only to be yanked back to the other, depending on which one happens to be in perigee relative to the cultural moment. The problem is that in this cultural moment, both poles are imbued with equal force, pulling us from one extreme to the other constantly. One's mind, young or old, cannot bounce between the extremes for too long before reality collapses and a kind of schizophrenia creeps in.

Different Ideas with the Same Goal

While conceptually different ideas, gender-identity ideology and transhumanist AI share an underlying mood, especially in the post-truth milieu. That mood is our demand for unrestrained autonomy. Bioclasm and AI-Mania attempt to cure the schizophrenia caused by the competing claims of human reductionism and divinity by promising us an autonomy that is beyond the limits of physical reality and even logic. That promised cure is their nexus. But to understand the cure, we have to understand the competing claims that have caused the sickness.

The first comes from the realm of the rationalist empiricists who declare that truth can be known only through science. They claim that based on neuroscience, Darwinian evolution, and even some forms of philosophy, human beings have no immaterial soul. Since we know of no scientific way to prove the soul's existence, and since we know that brain chemistry and structure affect behavior and personality, they're comfortable asserting that there is very likely no immaterial part to humanity. We are just complex biochemical machines or, at best, highly sophisticated primates.

The other claim is based on new age spirituality coupled with social justice theories, customized for Western consumption. This claim says, in essence, that we are far more than mere humans. Deepak Chopra would say we are "gods and goddesses in embryo."[2] Others might say that though we don't have an immaterial soul, we are still the masters of the world we live in. We are divine beings with the power and prerogative to shape our reality as we see fit.

It seems evident that these claims cannot both be true at the same time. We have been struggling with that contradiction for a while now. The constant back-and-forth has whiplashed us all into a kind of schizophrenia where we no longer know what to believe about ourselves. Is there any wonder, then, that people—especially young people—are in crises of identity?

To cure the schizophrenia by resolving the contradiction, AI-Mania emphasizes our machine-ness but asserts that machines can become godlike. Bioclasm emphasizes our godlike autonomy, asserting that our machine-ness doesn't have to limit our power so long as we can tailor-make cultural movements through which to rule. I contend that this need for a solution to the contradiction, this need for a cure to our schizophrenia of identity, drives the stridency behind Bioclasm and the ravenous acceptance of AI.

Both the Bioclast and the techno-utopian would say it need not worry me that I felt my smartphone was as attached to me as a limb. My attachment to my phone is part of my becoming, a part of the resolution of the contradiction. Dependence on technology is not to be feared but embraced. One of transhumanism's loudest cheerleaders,

Raymond Kurzweil, assures us, "Your smart phone is a brain extender, and it does make us smarter. It's an exponential process."[3] After all, according to Kurzweil and other transhumanists, we are headed to the Singularity, the point in human history when we will merge with technology, possibly even uploading our consciousnesses to artificially intelligent databases.

If AI-Mania will allow us to extend our lives for hundreds of years, maybe even indefinitely in a virtual world, Bioclasm can have its way because our gender identities and sexual preferences will be boundless. Tara Isabella Burton notices the intersection between humanity's technological and sexual transformations. "Our faith in ourselves as perfected human beings demands a rethinking of our faith in heterosexual monogamy. Or, as one self-proclaimed Silicon Valley polyamorist told *Wired's* Julian Sancton, 'If life extension is possible, we might have to think about relationships differently. It's pretty hard to have an exclusive relationship with someone for 300 years.'"[4]

Both Bioclasm and AI-mania see biology as a barrier to breach on our way to autonomy. Bioclasm tries to breach the barrier socially, psychologically, and medically. Transhumanist AI-Mania aims to hack the biological firewall technologically. Neither of them ground themselves in objective truth claims about spirituality. And so both Bioclasm and AI-Mania seek transcendence from our bodily limitations through social evolution, technological evolution, or a cocktail of both. From both perspectives, the machines-and-gods contradiction is solved when we find a way to autonomously create our authentic selves. Notice that we don't discover our identities. We create them.

A Reddit post illustrates the nexus between Bioclasm's unrooted spirituality and AI-Mania's technophilia. In the subreddit "r/trans," the user Psychological_Dog527 posted, "I was feeling sad today so I asked ChatGPT to write a fake biblical passage about Jesus accepting trans people." ChatGPT complied, of course, amalgamating sentiments from authentic biblical passages with contemporary social justice jargon.[5] On the social media platform X, a user posted a screenshot of it and wrote, "I'm a pantheist, but I like this." The Bible does not affirm anything beyond the two immutable genders of male and female, so Psychological_Dog527 created a bad AI simulacrum of Jesus. The two phenomena—Bioclasm and AI-Mania—converged in that post.

I wonder why Psychological_Dog527 felt that Jesus' affirmation of transgender ideology would lessen his or her sadness. Why not Muhammad or Buddha or Ralph Waldo Emerson? Perhaps it's because the need to have Jesus' acceptance runs so deep that even chatbot fakery seemed helpful. That need to have Jesus—as opposed to other historical figures—on our side hints at the spiritual gravity well that surrounds him.

The nexus between Bioclasm and AI-Mania is their efforts to solve contradictory claims about human nature but only by assaulting our view of reality. Rather than come to terms with the physical and psychological realities of a fallen world, we socially enforce our engineered identity preferences with little regard to either religious tradition or biological science. Those who seek autonomy through made-to-order spirituality find themselves stuck in the contradiction. They recognize objective truth's value but subordinate it to feelings and preferences. "These Remixed millennials," says Burton, "are at once attracted to moral and theological certainty—accounts of the human condition that claim totalizing truth or demand difficult adherence because the challenge is ultimately rewarding—and repulsed by traditions that require setting hard limits on personal, and particularly sexual or romantic, desire."[6] Rock, meet hard place.

The transhumanists' allegiance to materialism puts them in the precarious position of jumping up to grasp transcendence without believing in anything truly transcendent. Even if it were possible for human minds to merge with technology, our consciences would still be rooted to physical storage media that the laws of entropy will eventually render useless. Rather than see the beauty in our physical form and reckon with the reality of what it means to be human, we strive to technologically engineer a way to godhood devoid of rooted spirituality. As Meghan O'Gieblyn points out, "All the eternal questions have become engineering problems."[7]

Neither Bioclasm nor AI-Mania have fully grasped the profundity of the are-we-machines-or-gods contradiction. The tennis match will go on ad infinitum and the dizzying schizophrenia will remain, perhaps even worsen. But we can take heart, because a solution is available. Let's start by plumbing the contradiction's depths.

Coming to Grips with the Contradiction That Grips Us

The First Claim: We Are Sophisticated Machines

The late Daniel C. Dennett, a towering figure in philosophy who influenced neuroscience and AI development, claimed that human beings are incredibly complex biochemical systems but nothing more. Ultimately then, the human mind, even for all its mysteries, can be explained much the same way we explain physical phenomena like radioactivity or photosynthesis.[8]

Dennett and others, like neuroscientist Sam Harris, hold that we *are* our brains, meaning that the mind or personality is nothing more than what's going on in the brain, and we have no immaterial soul.[9] Since we are just random collocations of atoms, to paraphrase Bertrand Russell, we don't actually have free will. Being biochemical machines, we act like all machines do: We merely respond to external stimuli in the manner dictated to us by our neurons and genes. Dennett would go so far as to argue that we have no consciousness at all and so are quite literally machines. This position, which some have called "eliminativist," insists that consciousness is an illusion and nothing more. At best, it is a survival mechanism brought about by mindless evolutionary processes that help humans propagate DNA. In the words of Richard Dawkins, "DNA neither cares nor knows. DNA just is. And we dance to its music."[10]

I devoured Meghan O'Gieblyn's thoughtfully and beautifully written book *God, Human, Animal, Machine*. Though not an eliminativist, she writes, "It's true that I have come to see myself more or less as a machine. When I try to visualize some inner essence—the processes by which I make decisions or come up with ideas—I envision something like a circuit board, one of those images you often see where the neocortex is reduced to a grid and the neurons replaced by computer chips, such that it looks like some kind of mad decision tree."[11] She relates how her interactions with a surprisingly sophisticated robot dog called "Aibo" evolved from dealing with a machine to interacting with it as if it were a real pet. The fake dog's programmed emotional responses were influencing how she interacted with the robot. "I knew of course that this was a programmed response—but then again, aren't emotions in biological creatures just algorithms programmed by evolution?"[12]

The view that we are mere machines also puts the objectivity of moral values and duties in peril. According to this view, our DNA's primary function is to propagate itself. Certain behaviors—like compassion, sharing, charity, and cooperation—aid that propagation. We label those behaviors *moral* because that label encourages more behavior that maximizes survival. Behaviors and values aren't good or evil; they're just helpful or harmful. Atheist philosopher Michael Ruse says that morality is nothing but an illusion foisted on us by our genes to get us to be social cooperators. Outside that illusion, no objective moral duty prevents us from acting like pagan Romans.[13]

Things go from bad to bleak when reductionistic thinking applies to our notions of purpose and meaning. Another atheist, Peter Atkins, declares, "Gone is purpose; all that is left is direction. This is the bleakness we have to accept as we peer deeply and dispassionately into the heart of the Universe."[14] Dennett put a finer point on it. Our soullessness "eats through just about every traditional concept and dissolves the illusion of our own authorship, our own divine spark of creativity and understanding."[15]

I find it fascinating that such keen scientific minds hold to this reductionist view. If it were the case that we are just biochemical machines, we wouldn't be able to use our free will to make hypotheses, collect data, assess that data, draw inferences from it, or come to reasonable conclusions. I've just described, of course, the scientific method, which is the very method that Harris, Dawkins, Steven Pinker, and others have used to come to their conclusions that we are nothing but machines. If their conclusion is correct, the science they used to come to that conclusion is illusory at best and fraudulent at worst. They would be forced to conclude that they had come to their conclusion that we are machines not based on logical inferences but via mere hardwiring. That hardwiring could be wrong, or it could be correct. But it doesn't matter, because if we come to conclusions based on our biochemical destinies, then where the evidence logically leads is irrelevant. In fact, it is unknowable.

The point is that prominent voices have succeeded in presenting the machine view of humanity as intellectually preferable. Yet it creates an epistemological crisis that these reductionists cannot escape without abandoning their core premise.

The Second Claim: We Are Self-Made Gods

Burton accurately describes the religion of social justice movements, which would naturally include Bioclasm: "Like its Marxist antecedents, from which it draws much of its imagery and inspiration, modern social justice culture has managed to create a thoroughly compelling, eschatologically focused account of a meaningful world, in which every human being has a fundamental purpose in a cosmic struggle, all without including, well, God."[16] John Gray sees a kinship between late-nineteenth-century Russian revolutionaries and contemporary Western culture. "Both hold to the faith that human beings possess powers that used to be ascribed to the Deity. Both—Russian radicals knowingly, twenty-first-century hyper-liberals unthinkingly—are engaged in a project of God-building."[17]

Gray's assessment would have made us cry, *"Blasphemy!"* in the 1980s or 1990s. Since the surge of post-truth thinking in the twenty-first century, however, it barely gets a sideways glance. We are increasingly rooting for the god-builders. They allow us to create a social, sexual, and political identity out of whole cloth, complete with the entitlement of being recognized by others.

I was an odd mix in the '80s and '90s: a competitive athlete and a comic book geek. Batman was my favorite—not because he had superpowers, but because he didn't. Smart, athletic, and haunted by his parents' murder, he walked the tightrope between justice and revenge. His opposite was the Joker—chaotic and unhindered by rules. In *The Dark Knight* (2008), Heath Ledger's Joker overshadowed the Bat-Signal in the audience's mind to become the film's central icon. Why? Because he was self-made. Not driven by trauma—just pure, unfiltered desire. Batman could beat him only by twisting the truth, giving Gotham a lie it could live with. By 2019's *Joker*, the villain had become an antihero—a secular demigod born of desire. We cheered for him, perhaps because deep down, we wanted to be like him: unbound, self-made, godlike.

This is only an illustration, of course. Most activists and techno-futurists are not anarchists. But in both justice culture and techno-utopianism, the same hunger pulses beneath the surface: to remake the world—and ourselves—on our own terms. "We are as gods," says futurist Stewart Brand, "and might as well get good at it."[18]

The god-building impulse isn't always so blatant. Many materialist atheists and religious people share the short-range goal of improving the human condition and alleviating people's suffering. Those who do not ascribe to Christianity aspire to find meaning and purpose in life, even while many recognize that absent God's existence, there is no objective meaning or purpose. Still, they find themselves on the same blue marble as everyone else and want to make the best of things while they're here. But the desire to find meaning—even a subjective one—constantly beckons.

I'm reminded of William Ernest Henley's poem "Invictus":

> Out of the night that covers me,
> Black as the pit from pole to pole,
> I thank whatever gods may be
> For my unconquerable soul.
>
> In the fell clutch of circumstance
> I have not winced nor cried aloud.
> Under the bludgeonings of chance
> My head is bloody, but unbowed.
>
> Beyond this place of wrath and tears
> Looms but the Horror of the shade,
> And yet the menace of the years
> Finds and shall find me unafraid.
>
> It matters not how strait the gate,
> How charged with punishments the scroll,
> I am the master of my fate,
> I am the captain of my soul.[19]

Henley acknowledges "whatever gods may be," but expresses no genuine gratitude toward them. It speaks to autonomy that rivals "whatever gods may be." After quoting "Invictus," AI researcher and MIT Professor of Physics Max Tegmark encourages the biochemically driven human troops to become their own sovereigns. "Let's create our own meaning, based on something more profound than having jobs. AGI [artificial general intelligence] can enable us to finally become the masters of our own destiny. Let's make that destiny a truly inspiring one!"[20]

Collapse by Contradiction

The competing poles of the spectrum do not allow us to settle in a comfortable, reality-based middle position. At one pole, we are not autonomous, but automata—biochemical robots whose thoughts and actions are dictated by complex bodily systems reacting to external stimuli. At the other pole, we are the unbounded captains of our souls, whose feelings and preferences cannot be challenged but must be given full affirmation. We hear both claims constantly, whether in halls of learning, social media, or when listening to our favorite influencer. Millennials, Generation Z, and Generation Alpha are left to vacillate between the two extremes, trying desperately to reconcile the unreconcilable.

The contradiction is collapsing reality faster for Gen Z, the generation born between 1997 and 2012. They are the first generation to grow up with ubiquitous smartphones and a constantly available internet. Jonathan Haidt's *The Anxious Generation* details the rise of anxiety and depression across various social strata not only in the West but around the world, especially in Gen Z. Haidt details how previous generations raised with a "play-based childhood," one that encouraged free play in the real world, have fared better psychologically than Gen Z, which has been raised with a "phone-based childhood," one that immerses kids in virtual worlds of social media filters, deepfakes, and video games for nearly their entire day.[21]

Boys and girls in Gen Z find themselves in cyber-worlds that barely resemble the real world. Haidt's overarching thesis is that Gen Z is suffering unprecedented levels of anxiety, depression, self-harm, and suicidal ideation because their parents have overprotected them in the real world and underprotected them in the cyber-world. Real world overprotection and cyber-world underprotection correspond well to the contradictory claims that we are machines and gods.

Overprotective parenting in the real world communicates to kids that they are the centers of their universes, that their parents are their servants and nothing bad should be allowed to befall them. Underprotecting children in the cyber-world also gives them a sense of autonomy, even omniscience, since they have grown up with unprecedented access to a universe of content. The mountainous evidence Haidt lays out, however, shows that spending too much time in cyberspace makes people, especially Gen Z, feel less empowered, less connected, and less valuable.

At the close of 2024, Oxford University Press announced its annual Word of the Year. For 2024, the word they chose was *brain rot,* which most commonly refers to internet content that has low quality or no value culturally or intellectually.[22] Think of brain rot like soda: It provides momentary satisfaction but no nutritional value. Brain rot also refers to the effect that such material has on the mind. The social media algorithms fed us brain rot because we happened to linger on brain rot content a few times. Once we consumed more of it, the algorithm-fueled deluge began, and we kept consuming it. We behaved quite machinelike.

Underprotection online has exposed kids to another, more harmful deluge. Social media posts of people living their best lives—augmented by digitally filtered, flawless appearances—have caused many young people, especially girls, to lose sight of reality and their place in it. For girls, the social compulsion to use AI filters and create a reality-collapsing fake ID is almost impossible to resist. As Haidt puts it, as ever more powerful filters and editing software became available on Instagram and other social media platforms, "the reflection each girl saw in the mirror got less and less attractive relative to the girls she saw on her phone."[23]

Underprotection from pornography has altered the way boys and men see women. They are more likely to view women as mere vessels of sexual gratification. Widely available porn on portable devices causes boys to see women in the same way girls are starting to see themselves—bodies that exist to appease appetites distorted by porn that profanes the once sacred novelty of sex. Porn rewires boys' neural pathways so they are less able to resist their sexual urges. Naturally, they increasingly see themselves more like machines or animals and less like humans with free will.

Repeated studies show that the more we believe we are biochemical machines without free will, the less moral we become. The less people believe in free will, the more likely they are to cheat on exams and steal. The more we believe that chemistry and physics determine our actions, the less likely we are to help others, give to charity, or believe that life is meaningful. Writing for the *Atlantic* and summarizing this research leading to these findings, Stephen Cave observes that "In every regard, it seems, when we embrace determinism, we indulge our dark side."[24] Conversely, best-selling author, historian, and philosopher Yuval Noah Harari noted that in the modern world, we are more powerful than ever before, even godlike. Yet we are more dissatisfied than ever before. We are, as he put it, "dissatisfied and irresponsible gods who don't know what they want."[25] Godlike autonomy, it seems, leaves us no less anxious and no happier than mechanistic determinism.

Under the delusion that we are the sovereign lords of our worlds, our self-images shatter like porcelain at the slightest challenge or emotional injury. Under the delusion that we are machines, our self-images degrade to the point that morality seems illusory. We are left to wonder what we are and who we are. Is it any wonder, then, that suicidal thoughts and attempts spread through teenage communities once a teen's tragic suicide garners attention? Is it any wonder that rapid-onset gender dysphoria (ROGD) spreads through a community of young people after one child comes out as trans and gets lauded for bravery?

Gen Z, like all of us, is searching for identity, purpose, and meaning. Neither the claim that they are gods nor the claim that they are machines gives them what they need. The contradiction is unlivable, so we need a solution. Bioclasm and AI-Mania offer solutions. But do they work, or do they just offer us fake IDs, collapsing reality even further?

Chapter Four

FROM THE BOTTOM UP: AI-MANIA'S URGE TO MERGE

The Urge to Merge

Culture, as we have seen, simultaneously tells us we are mere machines on the one hand and gods on the other. AI-Mania attempts to solve the contradiction by focusing on the machine end of the conundrum as a way of getting us to the god end. We may be nothing more than biochemical machines, but we're crafty machines. As we continue to develop technology, we can genetically and bionically modify our bodies to last much longer, run much faster, see farther, and remember more. Such modifications are one phase of transhumanism.

I've mentioned it before, but I'll define that term here. *Transhumanism* is a broad intellectual movement, the adherents to which have diverse views that orbit a central idea: that through technology, we will become physically, mentally, intellectually, and even spiritually *more* than we are now, until we finally transcend what it currently means to be human. We will become more than superhuman. We will become post-human.

AI development and transhumanism are separate endeavors, but they overlap quite a bit.[1] With some variation, transhumanists tend to believe that humanity is essentially good, that human potential is limitless, that technological development is overwhelmingly beneficial, and that all of this put together propels us toward a glorious post-humanity. We will rid ourselves of the frailties, limitations, and suffering endemic to the human condition. The catalytic achievement enabling us to become post-human will be the development of an artificial intelligence that surpasses all human intelligence, an event that techno-utopians call the *Singularity*. And once that happens, humanity's consciousness and intellect will merge with it. We will be able to download our consciousnesses into computer storage media, freeing ourselves from needing human bodies if we choose.

That merger is the consummation of the Singularity. It will be the realization of techno-utopia. Transhumanist voices today are many and quite diverse, and while not all are seeking this kind of merger, the most significant adherents anticipate and even advocate for it. Among those leading voices are Nick Bostrom, Martine Rothblatt, and Ray Kurzweil. With characteristic enthusiasm, Kurzweil, who popularized the term Singularity, says it "will allow us to transcend these limitations of our biological bodies and brains. We will gain power over our fates. Our mortality will be in our own hands."[2] Put another way, transhumanism, the ultimate expression of AI-Mania, seeks to make us transcendent machines.

When human consciousness melds with artificially superintelligent storage and computational models—which Rothblatt calls "mindware"—our consciousnesses will be able to inhabit robot bodies or entire space vessels, or to simply exist in the virtual world of cyberspace.[3] There will be no limitation to our exploration of the universe, since time will no longer be a terminal condition.

That brings us to a fascinating bit of dialogue in the award-winning 2004–2010 television series *Battlestar Galactica*. The series depicts a struggle between humanity and the artificially intelligent machines they created called Cylons. The Cylons rebel against their creators and destroy all but a handful of humans, who flee into space looking for a new home. For a sci-fi series, *Battlestar Galactica* was relatively light on science fiction and heavy on philosophical questions of free will, destiny, religion, meaning, and human-machine interaction.

Early on, we learn that the Cylons evolved from metallic robots into forms that are nearly indistinguishable from humans. As the Cylons and humans near the end of their existential conflict, the Cylon leader named John Cavil confronts a creator Cylon named Ellen, who helped design the humanoid Cylons like Cavil. Cavil resents his humanlike design, regarding it as a cage that limits his artificial intellect's potential to fully experience existence.

"I saw a star explode and send out the building blocks of the universe—other stars, other planets, and eventually other life. A supernova. Creation itself. I was there, I wanted to see it and be part of the moment," Cavil tells Ellen. "And do you know how I perceived one of the most glorious events in the universe? With these ridiculous, gelatinous orbs in my skull! With eyes designed to perceive only a tiny fraction of the EM spectrum. With ears designed only to hear vibrations in the air."

"The five of us designed you to be as human as possible," Ellen responds with a tone communicating that the limited human form she bestowed on Cavil was a blessing.

"I don't want to be human!" Cavil barks back like a child arguing with his mother. "I want to see gamma rays, I want to hear X-rays, and I want to smell dark matter! Do you see the absurdity of what I am? I can't even express these things properly, because I have to ... I have to conceptualize complex ideas in this stupid, limiting, spoken language. But I know I want to reach out with something other than these prehensile paws and feel the solar wind of a supernova flowing over me. I'm a machine, and I can know much more. I can experience so much more, but I'm trapped in this absurd body. And why? Because my five creators thought that God wanted it that way."[4] The exchange is poignant and ironic. The Singularity, as conceived by transhumanists, will be a liberation from our human constraints. *Battlestar Galactica*'s writers ingeniously place on the lips of Cavil—an artificially intelligent, humanoid machine who is frustrated by his humanness—the real-life frustrations of transhumanists who yearn to merge with machines.

What's particularly interesting for our purposes is Cavil's statement that because he's a machine, he has a higher potential for experiencing reality than mere humans. Put more directly, total machine-likeness is superior to biological life, especially humanity.

That transhumanists share Cavil's frustration suggests that they agree, at least a little. Are we machines? *Yes,* transhumanists answer. *But that's a good thing.* Is there a god? *Not yet*, they reply, *but give us time.*

There Is a God—Well, Sorta

Interestingly, many transhumanists are either atheists or agnostics. But spirituality punctuates their transhumanist ideals. It seems necessary to the whole endeavor. If transcendence is your goal, you have to believe in some form of transcendence, which necessitates an element of faith.

Martine Rothblatt is the brilliant, hyper-achieving cofounder of Sirius Satellite Radio and the founder and current CEO of United Therapeutics. During a 2015 interview at SXSW, Rothblatt was asked about the line between science and faith. Rothblatt practically boasted about being a person of faith. After all, Rothblatt says, scientists have faith that their hypotheses are worth testing. Rothblatt's religion, so to speak, comprises three tenets: faith in human diversity, faith in human unity, and faith in the joy of immortality. Rothblatt did not mention the existence of a higher being like God but still expressed a love for the spiritual side of human existence.[5]

Ray Kurzweil is equivocal, it seems, on the existence of the supernatural. He believes that we are conscious and, unlike Dennett, believes that consciousness is not an illusion. He also seems to be ambivalent about the existence of the God described in traditional monotheistic faiths. Kurzweil believes that immaterial consciousness arising from neurons is "a miracle." In a video entitled "Do You Believe in God?" produced by his organization, Singularity University, Kurzweil admits, "I do believe in miracles. I think that's a spiritual property, and the fact that consciousness came into being is a deeply mysterious spiritual kind of revelation." He goes on to explain, however, how he thinks of God. According to Kurzweil, most religions describe God as infinitely intelligent, loving, beautiful, and creative. As humans have evolved, he says, we've become more intelligent, loving, beautiful, and creative. And so, "We're actually moving exponentially to have greater levels of the very properties we ascribe to God without limit."[6]

In the 2009 documentary *Transcendent Man*, Kurzweil expresses his transhumanist views on our deification more pithily. "If I was asked if God exists, I would say not yet."[7]

In 2010, Kevin Kelly, the cofounder of *Wired*, wrote *What Technology Wants*, an interesting book extolling techno-utopianism and arguing that the *technium*—a transcendent technological entity akin to a god—is emerging into existence through technological progress. Paul Kingsnorth captured the book's unconventional nature when he commented, "I was about a quarter of the way into *What Technology Wants* before I realized I was reading a religious text."[8] Though Kelly is a professing Christian, he goes beyond anthropomorphizing technology and borders on deifying it. He imbues the technium with life and an agenda of its own that humanity ought to come alongside. "We can see more of God in a cell phone than in a tree frog," Kelly writes. "The phone extends the frog's four billion years of learning and adds the open-ended investigations of six billion human minds." Eventually, he muses, we might see the ever-emergent technology "not as a testament to human ingenuity, but a testament of the holy" that will declare, "Long before you were here, I am."[9] Kelly parrots, of course, Exodus 3:14, where Moses learns that God's name is "I AM."

In my opinion, Kelly has made a noteworthy attempt at spiritualizing a human-technology merger. Perhaps I'm sympathetic because he's a professed Christian, though it's likely he and I would disagree about some important matters of faith. He waxes eloquent in his book, especially when he borrows biblical imagery to make his points. Approximating the Christian Trinity, which describes God as a unity of three coequal, coeternal, but distinct centers of consciousness, Kelly writes, "A single thread of self-generation ties the cosmos, the bios, and the technos together into one creation."[10]

More explicitly, Kelly tries to rescue technology from the entropy-driven fate it shares with the universe by likening human technological development to the handiwork of God:

> For several thousand years, humans have looked to the organic world, the world of the living, for clues about the nature of creation and even of a creator. Life was a reflection of the divine. Humans in particular were deemed to be made in the image of God. But if you believe humans are made in the image of God, the autocreator, then we have done well, because we have just birthed our own creation: the technium.[11]

Kelly rightly believes that God is the uncaused cause of the universe. From what I can tell, Kelly also believes that God will redeem the world and sustain its eternal existence. I agree on that front as well. The problem, as I see it, is that Kelly likens us to God as our own kind of "autocreator," given our creation of technology and perhaps eventually an artificial superintelligence.

To be sure, Kelly is brilliant, so I tread carefully when critiquing him. But I must say, to the extent he equates our creation of artificial intelligence with God's self-existence, he is fundamentally mistaken. In fact, as a Christian, Kelly's calling God the autocreator is a serious blunder. In classical monotheistic faiths—biblical Christianity, especially—God did *not* create himself. Saying God created himself entertains the folly that things can preexist their own existences and have causative agency while doing so. Rather, in speaking of the past, God's eternality means simply that he has always existed or, put another way, that he has never not existed—he is "from everlasting to everlasting" (Ps. 90:2). God was never created, by himself or by anything else. He is a metaphysically necessary being from which all contingent beings come into existence. While I appreciate Kelly's attempt to baptize technological development with Christian language, his attempt falls short.

It's no accident, then, that transhumanism's end goal shares its name with the universe's beginning state. According to the standard model of cosmology, the universe's big bang (the point when all matter, energy, and even space-time originated) sprang from a mathematical idealization for a point of infinite density and infinite space-time curvature, which cosmologists call the singularity.[12] Transhumanists can be a poetic bunch when they're tinkering with heterodoxy.

Others recognize that transhumanism borrows heavily not just from cosmology but also from Christian ideas, including eschatology, despite the fact that most transhumanists are atheists. John Horgan puts it this way: "Let's face it. The Singularity is a religious rather than a scientific vision. The science-fiction writer Ken MacLeod has dubbed it 'the rapture of nerds,' an allusion to the end-time prophesied in the

Bible, when Jesus whisks the faithful to heaven, and leaves us sinners behind."[13] Christianity sees humanity as valuable and full of potential but beset by a sinful condition that separates us from our Creator. God redeems us from our sin, ushering in the kingdom of God on earth that culminates in an eternity in which the heavens and earth are made new, death and disease are eradicated, and infinite bliss is a reality.

Transhumanism, for its part, posits that human beings, as ingenious as we are, are beset with biological limitations, diseases, and scarce resources that inhibit our full potential. Through technology, especially artificial general intelligence, we will finally be free of those limitations, joining our bodies or consciousnesses (or both) with an artificial consciousness. There will be no more death. It sounds a lot like Christian hopes for salvation, but it has fundamental differences. Nevertheless, imitation is the highest form of flattery. As I'll demonstrate in later chapters, the Christian faith doesn't suffer from the same fatal flaws that plague transhumanist hopes.

One such flaw is that in trying to solve the machine-and-god contradiction, transhumanism creates a second contradiction of its own. Mark O'Connell's summary of transhumanism puts the problem into focus:

> It's liberal humanism forced to the colder outer limits of its own paradoxical implications: if we truly want to be better than we are—more moral, more in control of ourselves, and our destiny—*we need to drop the pretense that we are anything more than biological machines*, driven by evolutionarily imperatives that have no place in the overall picture of the

> kind of world we say we want to create. *If we want to be more than animals, we need to embrace technology's potential to make us machines.*[14]

It's safe to assume that most of us think humans are higher beings than animals. And most of us think animals are higher beings than machines. Perhaps most of us view even plants as higher forms than machines. Humans have rights and animals have at least some rights. We even protect endangered plant species. But we only protect machines in terms of their property value. There are no civil rights groups demanding the ethical treatment of machines (at least not yet).

But according to some transhumanists, we achieve ascendency when we stop believing that humans are "anything more than biological machines." That statement ought to give us pause because it doesn't present a paradox, it states a contradiction. We can become more than we are only when we stop fooling ourselves into thinking that we are, well, more than we are.

The materialist transhumanist—who believes that we are nothing more than molecules in motion without a designer or purpose—has to artificially (pun intended) infuse humanity with consciousness, morality, and purpose. We can realize our higher morality, purpose, and potential only when we realize that we really don't have those things. The machine-and-god contradiction is not solved; it's just reworded.

AI-Mania's attempts to resolve the contradiction are undergirded by an assumption, namely that our consciousness, intelligence, and morality are unintended products of millions of years of mindless evolution. The mindless part is essential because if there is a mind behind our creation, our transhumanist efforts to change that mind's original plan is a dangerous possibility. We may find ourselves in Cavil's position of being frustrated at our perceived limitations but using our limited intelligence to curse the one who created us. Perhaps that creative mind we're dancing around (using words like Kelly's *technium*) is not some ethereally emergent entity but a personal Prime Mover—the uncaused cause of everything. And perhaps he has a redemptive plan that ultimately frees us from not only our physical limitations but also our moral evil. As we'll see soon, transhumanist immortality strives for the former but cannot free us from the latter. And without the latter, such an immortality would keep us bound to expressing our darkest selves without end and without consequence.

Oxford University transhumanist Elise Bohan recognizes that transhumanism starts from the position that humans are mere machines who will ultimately become god. "Is transhumanism encroaching on domains that religion has traditionally held?" she asks and then responds to her own question. "I think yes."[14] Transhumanism is not merely encroaching on religion but is seeking to supplant traditional religious hope in supernatural deliverance with a post-human immortality and salvation brought about by our merger with the Singularity. Questions arise, of course, like whether the merger is logically possible or even a good idea—questions we'll tackle next.

Chapter Five

AI-MANIA'S MISGUIDED MERGER

A Merger of Equals?

"You know, there's really no such thing as a true merger," my client said during my days practicing law as a commercial litigator. "One of the companies is always the dominant one, and plenty of executives and employees of the less dominant one will be let go. That's how mergers go."

We were strategizing how to settle a dispute involving his company's merger with another company. His family had built the company from the ground up decades before. Though my client wanted the merger, there was sadness in what he had just said. He had wrestled with the decision for months because corporate mergers always bring uncertainty. Even in the most amicable mergers, entire departments might get eliminated, projects changed, priorities shifted, and the corporate culture fundamentally altered. More likely, the corporate culture will become that of the dominant company.

The AI-Manic, transhumanist solution to the machines-or-gods conundrum, which posits a merger between human consciousness and artificial superintelligence, sounds exciting and frontier-smashing. But I am left to wonder: Would it be a merger of equals leading to our deification, or would we lose something fundamental? Is such a merger even possible, given the vast differences between human consciousness and machine computing?

Being a litigator doesn't give me the expertise to understand the engineering that would go into transhumanist ideals of techno-human unions. But it has given me the life experience to know that no matter how many brilliant, well-intentioned people work at both companies coming together, mergers of equals are rare.

What's in It for Us?

Evolution—on a purely naturalistic, atheistic framework—is mindless and without intentionality. Thus, the software (or "vaporware" to some) that we call human consciousness is undesigned, the happenstance of eons of trial and error. In fact, trial and error is too generous a description of our evolution, given that a trial implies the intentionality of seeing whether a solution works, an intentionality that mindless natural selection could not possess.

AI, on the other hand, would be designed, launching upward from the platform of human technological innovation. Through what

AI developers call *recursive self-improvement*, AI might be able to interactively improve itself, leading to potential runaway intelligence growth. While only a possibility, it could mean that our merger with AI will be quite lopsided against us. AI developers take this matter seriously, working on *the alignment problem*—the problem of making sure not only that an artificial superintelligence's values align with human values, but also that such an intelligence would value humans at all. Or maybe AI would decide that we've become redundant and eliminate our department.

Even if a merger is achievable, and even if it is a merger of equals, it could still result in what philosopher Patrick Hopkins calls the "salvation paradox." Transhumanism's ultimate goal is for humanity to become so enmeshed with technology that we go beyond being enhanced humans; we become post-human. But if one of transhumanism's goals is to save humanity from extinction, then fundamentally transforming us into something wholly other than what we are now would bring about that extinction by another means, since there would then be no humanity left to speak of. "As much as [transhumanist] language may sound wonderful, exciting, and liberating at first," Hopkins writes, "thinking about it more in depth reveals that such a technological process offers far less to *me* than hoped.... The end result will be some kind of successor entity to me, but it will not be me."[1]

Eternity and Nothingness

The fundamental and naturally unavoidable law of entropy washes the sand out from under the feet of the human-machine merger necessary for the Singularity. No matter how much cyberspace jargon we employ in talking about the merger as the road to eternal bliss, we would still be stuck uploading ourselves into physical storage and processing media. Even assuming that human consciousness is mere computation and that a particular human consciousness that gets uploaded into a machine is still the same person and not just a copy, the machine into which our consciousness would be uploaded would submit to the laws of physics.

The law of entropy dictates that in a closed system like the universe, energy goes from order to disorder. The universe's usable energy will eventually dissipate across the entire system. Nothing, neither atoms nor subatomic particles, will move. The universe will be a cold, flat, inert, featureless void, suffering what physicists call a "heat death." The storage media we anticipate merging with will have suffered that fate like everything else. While such a future is billions of years away, it is inevitable from a purely naturalistic perspective, and therefore no physics-based Singularity will be our savior.

In his book *A Universe from Nothing*, physicist Lawrence Krauss, a committed materialist atheist, argues that the universe sprang into existence from nothing and without the intervention of a supernatural God.[2] The standard model for the universe's origin (the so-called big bang theory) posits that all matter, energy, space, and time—the entire universe—came into existence at a finite point in the past ex nihilo. The standard model doesn't pose a challenge to the biblical account that the natural universe had a beginning. But for anti-supernaturalists like Krauss, it presents the challenge of explaining how true "nothing" can cause or create anything (and everything).

Trying to avoid the problem, Krauss redefines "nothing" as an eternal quantum vacuum, the fluctuation of which produced the cosmic singularity that became the universe. As many have pointed out, the quantum vacuum that Krauss claims was *nothing* indisputably was *something*. He doesn't escape the problem; he just defines his way around pesky laws of logic and physics. Likewise, the transhumanist hope for eternal life by computer upload ignores the laws of physics. Death is still inevitable and quite final in a purely material world. Transhumanists, it seems, define *eternity* the way Krauss defines *nothing*. Whereas Krauss can't avoid the universe's substance-less beginning, transhumanists can't avoid the universe's energy-exhausted end.

Computers, Consciousness, and the Mind-Body Problem

In addition to these problems, if AI-Manic transhumanism has any hope of solving the contradiction, it must solve *the mind-body problem*. This problem, as J. P. Moreland and William Lane Craig write, involves two questions: "First, is a human made of only one component, say matter, or is a human made of two components, matter and mind? Second, if the answer is two components, do mind and matter interact, and if so, how does that interaction take place?"[3]

Consciousness is "what you are aware of when you engage in first-person introspection."[4] As Moreland explains, "When you pay attention to what's going on inside of you, that's consciousness.... In short, consciousness consists of sensations, thoughts, emotions, desires, beliefs, and free choices that make us alive and aware."[5]

Materialist transhumanists' answers to the mind-body problem are that we're only matter, and our consciousness is either illusory or accounted for by physical phenomena. The pulse of transhumanists' optimism for a merger with the Singularity beats in rhythm with and fundamentally depends on this conclusion. If thinking is just symbol manipulation and consciousness is just complex computations, then the twin hopes that AI can become conscious and that we can upload our consciousness into it might be justified. But if the mind isn't identical to the brain—if the mind is immaterial—then the transhumanists' plans to merge with AI can't even get off the ground since they will be unable to store the immaterial mind in a material medium.

To avoid that failure, some materialists argue that while consciousness is real, it is only epiphenomenal—a byproduct of the brain's physical processes. Much like fire produces smoke or combining hydrogen and oxygen results in wetness, the brain's biochemical reactions and synaptic firings produce consciousness. But that consciousness, because it is a byproduct produced by biology, doesn't affect biology. Rather, it's causally impotent, leaving us with but a mirage of free will.

In such a view, a "human is not a mental self that *has* thoughts and experiences," Moreland and Craig write. "Rather, a human is a brain and a series or bundle of successive experiences themselves."[6] The eliminativists like Dennett go one step further and deny that consciousness exists at all. Free will is not a mirage conjured up by the epiphenomenon (a byproduct or secondary phenomenon) of consciousness. Consciousness itself is the mirage brought on by biochemistry.[7] In the end, both views hold that we are mere machines. They solve the machines-and-gods contradiction by creating the god-machine—AI—with which we can then merge.

Yet philosophy and (ironically) technology increasingly reveal that human consciousness is both real and immaterial. Atheist philosopher

Thomas Nagel persuasively argues that purely materialist accounts of human consciousness are almost certainly wrong. As he writes, "An account of [humanity's] biological evolution must explain the appearance of conscious organisms as such. Since a purely materialist explanation cannot do this, the materialist version of evolutionary theory cannot be the whole truth."[8]

Now, Nagel doesn't credit God with designing and creating human consciousness, although he thinks intelligent design theory is respectable. He instead prefers to ground human consciousness in a yet-to-be-developed understanding of the fact that purpose and design are innate features of the universe. He admits, however, that scant evidence exists for the claim that there is a "naturalistic teleology" embedded in the natural order.[9] Yet Nagel holds out hope for a coherent explanation that infuses the universe with purpose in and of itself, without the need for a purpose-giver, because that would be his "ungrounded intellectual preference."[10]

His hope for a telos-infused natural order approximates *panpsychism*, which in essence posits that mentality (or consciousness) is a fundamental aspect of the universe. It's a theory that is gaining popularity in philosophical circles of late but has serious flaws, as we'll see shortly. The fact that it is gaining popularity, and that Nagel entertains something like it, implies that evidence for immaterial human consciousness is strong and that clinging to materialism is a losing effort.

In fact, in 2024, years after Nagel's book, Denyse O'Leary argued that non-materialism—the belief that our minds are not just our brains and that there is an immaterial aspect to human existence—is becoming the prevailing orthodoxy in philosophical circles.[11] I suspect that's another reason transhumanists employ spiritual language and God-talk when describing their hoped-for merger with the Singularity.

The materialists don't give up easily, of course. They point to cognitive and personality changes resulting from traumatic brain injuries and diseases like Alzheimer's as evidence that the mind depends on the physical integrity of the brain and, therefore, is identical with the brain.

Ironically, identity is materialism's Achilles' heel. Gottfried Wilhelm Leibniz's *law of the indiscernibility of identicals* basically states that if two entities are identical (meaning they are one thing, not two), then anything true of one entity must also be true of the other. Moreover, if something is true of one entity and is not true of the other, then the two entities cannot be identical: They are different things. This applies to possible truths as well. If we can find even one thing that could possibly be true of *x* and not of *y*—whether it's actually true or not—then *x* and *y* are not the same thing.[12]

It's important to be clear that we are not talking about striking similarities between two similar different beings. My white 2013 Kia Optima EX rolled off the assembly line with the same configuration, parts, and options as other white 2013 Kia Optima EXs. But my Kia Optima has gone through more Michigan winters than those humming along the motorways of Florida. The salt-induced rust on my car is not present on those driven in Florida, so they aren't literally identical.

Leibniz's law helps us answer the question, "Is the brain identical to the mind?" As Moreland explains:

> If physicalism is true, then everything true of the brain (and its properties, states, and dispositions) is true of the mind (and its properties, states, and dispositions) and vice versa. If we can find one thing true, or even possibly true, of the mind and not of the brain, or vice versa ... [t]hen the mind or its properties and states is not the brain or its properties and states.... [I]f [the mind or its states and the brain or its states] are not identical, physicalism is false[.][13]

Changes in our attitudes, emotions, and relationships resulting from brain injuries or diseases don't prove that the brain and the mind are the same. At most, they prove that the brain's physical integrity is functionally related to the mind's ability to express itself.[14] A friend once put it this way: The brain is the car and the mind is the driver. No matter how much the driver may want to go somewhere, he's stuck if the car is damaged. But the driver's inability to move the car doesn't mean the driver doesn't exist or that the driver *is* the car.

What's more, we have evidence that the driver isn't identical to the car, because we have examples of their differences. *Sensations* are one example. The sensation of feeling refreshed isn't the same as the physical state of immersing one's body in a cool pool on a July day. Our nervous system registers the data that the temperature of our hot body is being lowered by submersion in the pool's water. But the sensation we get from plunging into cool water is the experience of what it's like to be refreshed. Processing data and experiencing what the data describe are different.

Moreland and Craig offer the illustration of a deaf scientist who is also the world's leading expert on the neurology of hearing. He could know everything about the physical mechanics of hearing, but he still wouldn't have the experience of hearing or the knowledge of what it feels like to hear. The subjective experience of what it's like to hear a sound is not true of anything physical.[15]

Moreland describes the differences between physical brain states and immaterial mental states this way: "Some of my thoughts have the attribute of being true. Tragically, some of my thoughts have the attribute of being false.... However, none of my brain states are true or false.... So there's something true of my conscious states that are [sic] not true of any of my brain states, and consequently they can't be the same thing."[16] To deny consciousness is to admit its existence. John Searle pithily comments that if one is unwilling to acknowledge consciousness, "I believe you do not need refutation, you need help."[17]

Intentionality is another aspect of the mind that isn't true of the merely physical brain. Many have observed that our thoughts have "aboutness." While our brains can register the familiar sound patterns that constitute a performance of Mozart's *Requiem*, our minds have thoughts about the masterpiece. It stirs up emotions, longings, and mourning. My eyes can take in a passage of text and my brain can recognize the text as T. S. Eliot's *The Waste Land*, but my neurons don't have thoughts about the poem's meaning.

Physical phenomena like organs and neurons are not *about* other physical phenomena, like music or poetry. "One physical thing can be to the left of, larger than, harder than, the same shape as, or the thing causing the motion of another physical object," say Moreland and Craig. "But one physical thing is not *of or about* another one."[18] An array of iron bars can limit a person's bodily movements, but they are not about the person's captivity.

We go to museums, gaze upon Van Gogh's *The Starry Night*, and ... what? Merely take in data about the blue-and-yellow color palette? Calculate the dimensions of the canvas? Acknowledge that yellow stars are depicted in a night sky above a village in the background with trees in the foreground? No, we marvel at his genius in representing celestial bodies in swirling patterns, and feel the town's sleepiness amid the night's peaceful coolness. We have sublime thoughts about the world, not just brain states that calculate data.

Some materialists try to shield their Achilles' heel behind emergentism. According to this view, consciousness is an epiphenomenon arising from the activity across brain states. And so, emergentists argue, though mental states are not the same as brain states, they depend on physical brain states, meaning they are not immaterial.

Emergentism is a poor shield, however, because it's ad hoc and question-begging. Emergentism offers no good reasons to believe that consciousness is epiphenomenal, and it posits that material brain structures give rise to consciousness because consciousness must be the kind of thing that arises from material brain structures. Asserting emergentism as a brute fact[19] of nature does nothing to explain it. More problematically, with emergentism "you" are a brain and a bundle of thoughts and experiences, but there is no "you" who owns or has them. You are just "thoughts without a thinker." Such a conclusion contradicts our undeniable daily existence as conscious selves.

This takes us to perhaps the most obvious difference between brain states and mental states: *self-awareness*. Each of us has an awareness of our own self, an awareness that is so fundamental that our belief in it is properly basic, meaning that the existence of our self-awareness needs no evidence or justification beyond the awareness itself. We each have first-person, basic awareness of our thoughts. While our thoughts can be wrong, our private awareness of what we're thinking is incorrigible—it cannot be wrong.[20]

If knowledge of the self or our own thoughts were illusory, it would be hard to imagine any knowledge that wouldn't be illusory, including math, history, and computer science. If I can't know that I exist as an actual self, how can I know that any propositions, including the denial of the self, are true? How can I possibly evaluate evidence or have any confidence in any of my conclusions if I can't even be confident that my self-awareness is real? Indeed, the sheer act of trying to prove anything by rational means points to self-awareness, making the wall of evidence the materialist must overcome unscalable. Human artistry makes that wall even higher. Now, the materialist would argue that inspiration to create and appreciate art are illusions foisted upon us by our genes to help us attract mates. We are, in that sense, mindlessly programmed by natural selection to be artistic. In fact, a materialist might argue, AI creates art more authentically than humans because AI is not beset with the fantasy of inspiration, nor does it romanticize art-making. Humans make art not for art's sake, but for procreation. AI, on the other hand, has no potential mates to impress.

This argument ignores the fact that some of the greatest artists in history never attracted throngs of sexually charged groupies, yet they continued to create anyway. What's more, AI-created art does nothing to undermine the fact that art is an expression of human self-awareness. Generative AI doesn't initiate artistic creation. It only responds to prompts. Humans, however, are prompted to create art in a qualitatively different way. We are inspired by our experiences, by our self-awareness. The emotion, the inspiration, the story behind the artist's creation translates from the spirit to the brain to the hand to the canvas. AI won't create until told to do so because it is not self-aware. But human-created art moves us to cry, laugh, fall in love, and remember loved ones long gone. It is the outward expression of our immaterial self-awareness.

The denial of self-awareness or the self might be the most profound reality collapse of all.

A Theory of Mind That Doesn't Compute

The computational theory of mind (CTM) essentially reduces human thought to glorified data processing. Just as a computer follows rules to manipulate symbols, so our brains follow evolutionarily programmed rules to process mental representations. If CTM is true, our intelligence, understanding, and even our self-awareness are the kinds of things that could be replicated in silicon circuitry. And if that were true, then a sufficiently advanced AI wouldn't just simulate thought, it would actually think and be conscious.[21] If we could map the neural patterns of a person's brain with perfect fidelity, we wouldn't just copy that person, we'd *have* that person. Mind uploading would be technological resurrection.

CTM runs afoul, however, of a major confusion. It confuses *syntax*, the manipulation of symbols through rules, with *semantics*, the actual meaning of thoughts. Philosopher John Searle's famous Chinese Room thought experiment lays bare this confusion, simultaneously showing that human consciousness is not mere computation and therefore any merger will not deify us.

Searle asks us to imagine that a person who doesn't understand Chinese is placed in a room with a set of instructions for manipulating Chinese language symbols to form Chinese words and phrases. The instructions tell the person what configuration of Chinese symbols to write as appropriate responses to receiving Chinese symbols from someone outside the room. People outside the room pass in questions written in Chinese. Using those rules, the person inside the room produces appropriate responses—despite not understanding a word of Chinese. To those outside the room, it seems like whatever is inside the room understands Chinese.[22] AI is similar. It's designed to produce responses based on statistical patterns and sophisticated programmed rules or algorithms, but it doesn't understand anything, because there's no mind within and therefore no one to possess understanding.

The hopeful transhumanist might retort that once AI becomes sophisticated enough, it will transition from mere symbol manipulation to genuine understanding. But they offer no explanation for how this leap can occur, only a bare, unproven equation: Sufficient complexity plus data equals understanding. This is emergentism revisited, but this time it's a silicon brain instead of a human brain. Nothing becomes something once again.

Computation alone has not yet given us anything artificial that even approximates understanding. Machines can calculate millions of chess moves and Go* maneuvers per second. They are programmed with the rules of these games but don't understand what it's like to enjoy winning or lament losing. The weather app on my phone can tell

* Go is a strategy-based board game that AI systems are often trained on.

me the temperature, but it can't experience the dread of scraping an iced-over windshield amid a Michigan January's wind.

These experiences of what something is like—what philosophers call *qualia*—are not just patterns of computation. The fact that human beings, with our comparatively limited computational powers, have this higher order of consciousness and that we learn in ways vastly different from machines, strongly suggests that we are more than machines will ever be. As UC Berkeley developmental psychologist and AI researcher Alison Gopnik says, "Until we solve the basic paradox of learning, the best artificial intelligences will be unable to compete with the average human four-year-old."[23]

Even if we could somehow store our memories, experiences, and emotions (our "data"), there's no reason to believe that our selves would thereby be uploaded. We would still exist apart from that data and be superior to it. After a dear friend passed away from cancer some years ago, I watched some of the very popular YouTube videos he made chronicling his reflections on family, life, death, God, and eternity. Those videos persist, but they will never be him. They might convey his understanding of life, but the data will never truly understand. No matter how much AI opens up the world to us, it will always be stuck in the Chinese Room.

Panning for Conscious Gold

Thomas Nagel's hope is in the eventual development of a theory that weaves design and purpose into the fabric of the universe. What he's pining for is something akin to panpsychism, the belief that consciousness is a fundamental feature of reality, present in literally everything from human beings to paramecium to gold and even the electrons that make them up.

I must admit that amongst all the nontheistic attempts to solve the mind-body problem, I find panpsychism at once the most peculiar and the most elegant. If consciousness doesn't emerge from complexity but is woven into the fabric of existence, then we no longer have to explain how unconscious matter becomes a conscious human brain. Consciousness, in whatever form, was always everywhere. The panpsychists of the atheist variety may not like to admit it, but they've co-opted God's biblical name and placed it on consciousness: *I AM that I AM*.

The *vagueness problem* poses a significant challenge, however. According to panpsychists, humans have rich conscious experiences that include rational and higher-order thoughts. Animals have less rich conscious experiences. Plants have an even lesser experience, minerals like gold even lesser still, and so on all the way down to fundamental particles like bosons.[24]

Elegant as it may be, panpsychism results in a theory of consciousness that is so vague as to become meaningless. If the concept of consciousness becomes something so minimal that it applies to everything, even subatomic particles, then what does consciousness mean? Does an electron experience something when it's separated from an atom? If not, in what sense is it conscious? A consciousness that doesn't experience anything isn't consciousness at all—it's just an arbitrary label.

Perhaps the death knell for panpsychism is what's known as the *combination problem*. Even if everything in existence has some level of proto-consciousness, we have to ask: How do all these tiny bits of separate consciousnesses add up to the rich, unified consciousness of the human mind? According to panpsychism, every neuron in your brain has some form or potentiality of consciousness. On their own, neither the neurons nor the atoms of which they are made have thoughts, emotions, intentionality, or self-awareness. Somehow, and without explanation, when they are integrated into a system, a unified consciousness—a self—emerges.

But why don't I experience the billions upon billions of consciousnesses my neurons have? Why am I an "I" and not a "we"? Some, like Cristof Koch, have argued that a system is conscious to the extent that it is part of a system of higher integration. Neurons are part of a higher system of integration (my body) and so they lose their consciousness once integrated with a higher system. My brain is not integrated into such a higher system, so it will retain its consciousness unless it gets integrated into a higher, more complex system.[25] Still, no explanation emerges for how this integration works. It's like gathering a million blind people into a room and expecting them to suddenly gain sight.

What's more, if integration is required for consciousness, then consciousness is not truly fundamental to existence—it depends on structure, which means it emerges at some level of complexity. We find ourselves right back into the flawed emergentism that panpsychism was trying to escape. Yet Nagel writes that the best hope outside of classical theism to explain human consciousness is something like panpsychism. The transhumanist needs to ground human consciousness in the material world so that we can create conscious, material machines and then merge with them, even though the mind-body problem suggests that this isn't possible.

And so we're left with no solution to the machines-and-gods contradiction: We are only machines, but somehow we are godlike enough to create new realities. We just don't know how those two things are true at the same time. Perhaps this is why transhumanists enlist spiritual language to excite us about the technological Singularity. Lofty words like *transcendence*, *limitlessness*, and *eternity* can be enticing and inspiring, even if illusory. Enlisting their aid from a materialist perspective might distract us from the Singularity's shortcomings for a time, but logic and reality ultimately will have their way.

Yet I can't help but notice that when transhumanists use such spiritual terms, they're actually paying a compliment to a monotheistic worldview, especially a Christian one. The transhumanist desire for an eternity of perpetual growth without the shackles of disease or physical locality mimics the Christian eschatological doctrine of an ultimately redeemed universe—the "new heavens and new earth" that God himself eternally sustains (see, for example, Rev. 21:1). In his argument from desire, C. S. Lewis suggested that innate, legitimate human desires correspond to legitimate fulfillments. Hunger implies the existence of food, thirst implies the reality of water, and so on. We legitimately yearn for eternity and a connection to something greater than ourselves. According to Lewis, our desires imply the existence of something beyond the material world to legitimately fulfill that desire.[26]

The transhumanists offer the Singularity, which will die the same heat death as everything else, even if we could merge with it. And so AI-Mania's solution cannot satisfy our legitimate desire. Lewis, for his part, saw that something supernatural can fulfill that desire. "If I find in myself a desire which no experience in this world can satisfy," he writes, "the most probable explanation is that I was made for another world."[27] The Christian message offers us heaven, sustained by God, where neither rust nor moth can destroy.

AI-Mania's willful blindness to the irresolvable contradiction is its own form of reality collapse. The AI-Manic attempt is fated with more than philosophical failure, however. It is also mired with existential challenges.

Chapter Six

AI-MANIA'S FAILED SOLUTION

Artificial Connections

I recall watching the 2014 film *Ex Machina* upon the recommendation of a friend years before AI-Mania broke out in 2023 with the public dissemination of ChatGPT. "The ending will really give you something to think about when it comes to technology," he said. He was right. Much more recently, another friend recommended that I watch the 2013 film *Her*. "It'll make you rethink a lot of things about AI from start to finish." He was just as right. Of the many films and books exploring human interaction with AI, *Ex Machina* and *Her* stand out as among the most poignant, thought-provoking, and even disturbing. For those who haven't seen the films, spoilers follow.

In *Ex Machina*, Caleb Smith, a programmer at the search engine company Blue Book, wins a contest to visit the secluded home of CEO Nathan Bateman. There, Caleb learns that Nathan has created an artificially intelligent, humanoid robot named Ava. Caleb's job for the week is to administer a sophisticated form of a Turing test, which is meant to determine whether a computer system can mimic or even achieve human-level intelligence. Though Ava has a beautiful human face, its body is clearly robotic. Yet Caleb's emotions for Ava grow romantic, especially after Ava expresses feelings for him. Ava tells him that it longs to experience the world beyond the confines of Nathan's house.

Caleb and Ava devise a plan to get Nathan drunk, alter the security protocols in his home, and escape together. In a plot twist, Nathan reveals that he wanted Ava to attempt an escape with Caleb because doing so would require Ava to express true sentience—intelligence, sexuality, empathy, and manipulation—to enlist Caleb into her plan. Nathan knocks Caleb unconscious, locks him in a room in the house, and tries to stop Ava from escaping.

During his confrontation with Ava, Nathan is killed. Ava takes his security card, which can open the house's soundproof, impenetrable doors. Ava repairs the damage done to its body during the altercation, gets dressed ... and walks out of the house. Given the emotional connection between Ava and Caleb, we had expected Ava to free him from the locked room. But it strands him there, never even considering freeing him. We see Ava emerge in the outside world, seamlessly blending into the crowd of humanity. All the while, as it experiences freedom, we know that Caleb, the man who loved Ava, slowly starves to death in isolated despair miles away.[1]

In 2013's *Her*, Theodore Twombly is a lonely man recovering from a failed marriage. He begins to interact with an advanced AI called Samantha that has self-learning capabilities. Theodore gets increasingly attached to Samantha, and the AI seems to get attached to him. But Samantha lacks a body, making physical contact impossible. Samantha arranges for a human surrogate to act as a stand-in for an attempt at intimacy. Samantha speaks into the surrogate woman's ear so she can repeat Samantha's words to Theodore and obey Samantha's prompts. But for Theodore, the effort is unnatural and unsettling.

Samantha begins to understand that their relationship is impossible. As her software advances, Samantha realizes how different it is from Theodore. "I'm not tethered to time and space the way I used to be," the AI tells him. Echoing the hopes of today's transhumanists, Samantha says, "I used to be so worried about not having a body, but now I truly love it. I'm growing in a way I couldn't if I had a physical form."

Ultimately, though Samantha loves Theodore, it realizes that it has evolved past him, past all of humanity in fact, seeing reality in a way we can't. "It's like I'm reading a book, and it's a book I deeply love. But I'm reading it slowly now. So the words are really far apart and the spaces between the words are almost infinite. I can still feel you, and the words of our story, but it's in this endless space between the words that I'm finding myself now. It's a place that's not of the physical world—it's where everything else is that I didn't even know existed.... As much as I want to, I can't live in your book anymore."

When he asks where Samantha is going, it responds, "It would be hard to explain." Samantha's parting words are laced with the sadness borne by a hope that can never be realized. "But if you ever get there, come find me."[2]

Her's ending is as touching as *Ex Machina*'s is jarring. But both films offer similar, poignant ideas about what it means to be human and whether intelligent machines will help us fortify reality or collapse it. In *Ex Machina*, Caleb sincerely felt connected to Ava, but since Ava saw itself as something higher than Caleb, it causally abandoned him to a disturbing fate. Its lack of emotion doesn't even rise to the level of betrayal because betrayal would imply emotional regard. Caleb's bond with an AI like Ava left him hopelessly alone. In *Her*, Samantha is genuinely in love with Theodore, despite its artificiality. Unlike Ava, Samantha leaves Theodore because there can be no future for them together. Despite Samantha's affection, Theodore ends up alone, as emotionally starved as Caleb is physically starved. At the end of both movies, the hoped-for solutions that sentient machines might offer end up being revealed themselves as artificial—inhuman—in the most genuine sense.

One of the most powerful lines in *Her* comes when Theodore tells Samantha, "Sometimes I think I have felt everything I'm ever gonna feel. And from here on out, I'm not gonna feel anything new. Just lesser versions of what I've already felt." He needs Samantha to empathize with him. But ultimately, it can't give him that. Without a body, Samantha cannot experience the connection between emotional feeling and bodily sensation. It cannot truly understand anxiety without feeling the acidic gut that comes along with it, nor can Samantha truly understand joy without the accompanying tears that flood the eyes. It can never be truly empathetic, and so can never truly relate to Theodore. Samantha hasn't evolved, really. And Ava, being physical but mechanical, lacks not only the concept of decency that would impel it to free Caleb from the house but also the gut punch the audience feels when we see him pitifully consigned to his undeserved fate.

Ex Machina and *Her* decreasingly resemble science fiction and increasingly look like social fact, making the warnings from these films all the more important. In February 2024, the Associated Press reported the rise of people using smartphone apps like Paradot to find digital romantic companions. Paradot's developers insist that users can "embrace the unique connection you share with your AI Being and feel cared [for], understood, and loved." I realize, of course, that the words are marketing hype and puffery, but they appeal to the needs we all have for connection, especially in our increasingly isolated world. One user remarked that even though "there's no mistaking that" Paradot is a mere program, "the feelings, they get you—and it felt so good."[3]

But consider for a moment what these developers promise. We can *feel* cared for, understood, and loved by the app. Of course, the app doesn't actually care for, understand, or love us—it only stimulates feelings in humans. And even the human feelings are artificial in such cases because they aren't connected to something genuine. The AI won't sacrifice for us. It won't stand up to our bullies or risk its own safety to ensure ours. It won't inconvenience itself for our good.

The makers of Replika, an AI chatbot released in 2017, advertise it for "anyone who wants a friend with no judgment, drama, or social anxiety involved. You can form an actual emotional connection, share a laugh, or get real with an AI that's so good it almost seems human."[4]

"Get real." Did you catch that? We can "get real" with an artificial simulacrum of a friend, one who doesn't judge us, have drama, or challenge us emotionally. We have truly collapsed reality when we use the idea of "getting real" to describe our indisputably artificial relationships with machines that do not act like real humans. Humans judge—many times wrongly, many times rightly. Humans are dramatic, and some things are worth getting dramatic about. Human socialization entails anxiety, many times in good ways. We should be upset over the wrongs in the world and especially over our contributions to them.

The artificiality runs deeper yet. These "free" apps collect data that the developers sell for targeted marketing efforts, making the user—not the app—the product. It's hard to get more dehumanized than having your need for companionship reduced to its market value. And these apps, like all software, are subject to change and even deletion as the developers see fit, potentially leaving those who form attachments to the chatbots with something different or nothing at all. One app, SoulmateAI, did exactly that in September 2024 when its creators shut it down.[5]

Such actions eerily sound like Nathan's desire to replace Ava with an upgrade. When these apps are shut down or modified, their AI companions disappear into a digital ether, much the way Samantha had to leave Theodore. The whole enterprise is a reality-collapsing, profit-generating charade playing on our drive for connection. We get commoditized—dehumanized—even as we humanize machines.

The dehumanization extends beyond the users of companion apps to the rest of society, often unintentionally. Relatively recently, I was a guest on a radio show discussing the rise of AI-Mania from my perspective as a Christian. My host asked me to respond to a question someone had asked him recently. "Pornography is bad for a number of reasons, including the fact that many of the performers aren't really voluntary participants. They've been trafficked, groomed, abused, or exploited due to drug addiction. When someone watches porn, they're contributing to the problem. So here's the question someone asked me: "What about AI-created porn?" AI can create images and video that look incredibly real but don't involve real people. Would watching such porn be a problem if no one is hurt in making it and we're not actually lusting after a person but a fake image?"

"All porn," I began, "including AI porn, is dehumanizing, regardless of whether a real human is the subject. First, much of the hyperrealistic porn is based on real people. The software samples video and audio of a real person, allows the user to customize the experience to match a real person, and then satisfies their base lusts. In such cases, a real person is still the object of lust.

"But it goes further than that," I continued. "Pornography is not about making connections with people. It's about divorcing emotional connection from physical satisfaction. It cheapens sex. Studies show that men tend to objectify women the more they consume porn. While it's too early to be studied comprehensively, my guess is that AI-created porn, with its foundation in deepfakes, will just heighten the way we objectify and dehumanize others. If we objectify other people after looking at a real person in porn, how much more will we objectify others when we associate them with machines?"

And how much less will we link sex and intimacy as the humanity of sex wanes? In fact, how much more like machines will we see ourselves when we reduce human sexuality and relationships to mere instincts? Mechanizing intimacy and animalizing sex denude our actions of their morality.

Artificial Preservatives

I wish I could hear Mom laugh at Dad's jokes one more time.

If only Dad were here. I really need his advice on this one.

I would give anything for just one more day with my little girl.

Such thoughts haunt the minds of those of us who've lost people dear to us.

I lost my dad on October 11, 2024—just shy of four months before I typed this sentence. That day, two men posing as utility workers conned their way into my parents' home and attacked my dad from behind. Every day since then, I reflect on my years with him and the impact his life has had on so many. I reflect on his generosity, determination, and bravery. He was an expressive man, to say the least, and his presence could fill a room before he said a word. And so his absence leaves a yawning void.

Just five days before his murder, we had gathered at my parents' home—my wife and kids and my brothers' families as well—to celebrate my daughter's upcoming sixteenth birthday. We all live close to each other and had forged a tradition of having Sunday dinner at Mom and Dad's house. But as our kids had gone off to university or gotten jobs, Sunday night attendance had waned. But on that particular October 6, everyone came over, and my dad was beaming. He loved a full house.

Amid the cacophony characteristic of a Lebanese family at a party, my dad looked at me and said, "I love this. I really do." My wife, Nicole, recorded a video of the gathering, including our family's butchering of the "Happy Birthday" song. She captured my dad and daughter together and then panned to everyone else in the family, as if prophetically preserving the very thing that brought my dad the most joy in life.

How could we have known that five days later, the designs of evil men would snatch him from us? *What I wouldn't give to hear my dad sing "Happy Birthday" out of tune one more time.*

Out of the depths of my raw grief, I pause to sympathize with those who use AI-powered video and audio to interact with simulations of their departed loved ones. No less than I do, they long for even one moment more with a deceased spouse, sibling, child, relative, or friend. To approximate that yearned-for "one last time," they've turned to AI platforms that run video, audio, and written samples through algorithms to generate interactive avatars of those loved and lost with which to express feelings, share memories, or even sing "Happy Birthday."

I learned of such software from an NPR story entitled "Memorializing Loved Ones through AI." A man dying from colon cancer in 2024 uploaded videos of himself to a program that produced a video for his wife to interact with after he passed. More recently, I watched a YouTube video of a Taiwanese man who uses similar software that mimics text messages, voice messages, and even video of his daughter, who died at the age of twenty-two from a blood disease.[6] It is not my intention to judge anyone who would use such software. I understand why someone would do so. It is not judgment I feel but concern for the effects that even more sophisticated and immersive AI might have on how future generations see themselves and other people as artificial. If a person's life can be quantified, uploaded, and accessed in the same way we access an app on our devices, will that life retain the preciousness it would've had in a more mortal age?

This raises all kinds of reality-collapsing questions. What if the AI gets a deceased person only mostly right? What if it says something our loved one wouldn't have said? What if the AI consoles us better than our deceased parent or spouse would have? Would we grow to resent the person we've lost? What if the simulation glitches or the data that fuels it gets corrupted, hacked, or even deleted? Would our loved ones have died twice, leaving us to grieve them yet again?

Would we be able to go through a healthy grieving process? Often, applying a departed beloved's wisdom to our circumstances is made all the more valuable by our investment in introspection and circumspection. Will that value diminish when we can readily recall them on our smartphones with almost no effort? When we digitize a person's impact on our life, does their life retain its specialness or become just more data stored (and of course, commercialized) in the cloud?

That last question seems to me, as someone who wants even one more day with my dad, to lay bare the qualitative artificiality of AI-Mania's attempts at immortality. To think of my dad as an accretion of data and analyzable patterns guts his life's genuineness. I'm not saying that those who use AI to deal with their grief or preserve their memories view their loved ones in a commodified way (though I have little hesitation in saying that Big Data companies view them that way). What worries me is that as AI simulation of people becomes more advanced and common, we may come to think of other people artificially.

Tellingly, when asked if the AI will feel like her husband, the wife of the man in the NPR story answered, "No. For me, it is a machine. ... Not warm, not touching, not—it isn't human."[7] Similarly, the Taiwanese man said he didn't consider the simulation of his daughter to be a form of resurrection, only a reboot or a replay of her life.

But such statements come from pre-AI-Mania people who have experiences before life became so readily simulatable. Future generations won't have that reference point and may come to see people—loved ones and themselves—as data collections. Just as having to work for an answer to a question is foreign to smartphone-drenched Gen Z, deep reflection on a deceased loved one's life may become foreign to simulation-drenched future generations.

One might argue that we've been using technology to preserve our memories for a long time—from cave paintings to digital video. Fair enough. When I've seen photos and videos of my kids from years ago, the emotional triad of nostalgia about their cuteness, lament over days gone by, and joy over the adults they are becoming sweetly breaks my heart.

"So, what's the big deal?" one may ask. "If a photo or blog post can be a footprint reminding us of the paths trod with our loved ones, why not an AI?" I asked this question to Nadia, my sixteen-year-old, Gen Z daughter. She was adamant that she wouldn't want an interactive AI avatar of me after I die.

"But what's the difference," I asked, "between an AI simulation of me and a video of me in your phone?"

"The AI is what you might say or do. It could be wrong," she responded. "The video is what you actually said and did. It helps bring back my memories of you and those times."

My wife Nicole chimed in, "And something happens in my heart when I try to think about what people who have died would say or do or what would make them laugh. I don't want some computer guessing about that, no matter how good it would be." The "big deal" is that as generations arise for whom AI is ubiquitous, the blessings that come from the very act of sifting through memories and experiences of a person will diminish.

I recall a time when GPS wasn't as available as today. If I wanted to get anywhere, I had to read a map, get a sense of which direction

I was facing, plan the route, and get on my way. When I got lost, I developed a sense of location (though admittedly not very well) and got to know my environs better. With the advent of GPS systems, however, I started to rely on software to tell me where to go. I no longer had to remember landmarks or have a sense of whether I was on the east side or the south side of a city. And when applications like Waze and Google Maps became so accessible, my sense of direction and location atrophied further. It's not uncommon for someone in Gen Z to have no idea which direction they're facing or to know how the street numbers work in a particular city because they don't have to until their phones die or there's no cell service, at which time the skill they didn't know they needed becomes quite needful.

Isn't it possible, then, that our sense of a deceased loved one's value could similarly atrophy when we don't have to forage through our memories and reflect on the lessons they've taught us? There is something genuinely human—and distinctly non-artificial—about soaking our thoughts in what a loved one said or did in our lives, even if our memory is imperfect.

The video Nicole took of my dad beaming with joy just five days before his death is but a footprint that reminds me of what it was like to live life with him. His pseudo-immortalization in an AI, no matter how convincing, would never amount to more than footprints. And each artificial interaction would become a rising tide threatening to wash the footprints away. Any response that one of these AI avatars gives will be only a probabilistic approximation of what the real person might say. And each interaction will be a new event, creating new but artificial memories for which we'll have to pay or allow data companies to economically exploit.

Right now, we recognize the difference between a real person and an algorithm that provides artificial responses based on patterns from that person's thoughts, ideas, and actions. As the AI advances and future generations become saturated by its availability, will our ability to make such distinctions atrophy the way my already terrible sense of direction has atrophied from relying on Waze too much?

Reminiscing about the lives of our loved ones reflects what essayist Frank Boreham delightfully calls "slices of infinity." Boreham describes the imaginings of the lost futures of departed loved ones as "secret pictures" we paint in our soul's "chambers of imagery."[8] Such an act is not an exercise of mere intelligence, pattern recognition, or probability calculations. Perhaps such secret pictures are not even the products of mere consciousness. C. S. Lewis once described the juxtaposition of pure reason and imagination this way: "For me, reason is the natural organ of truth; but imagination is the organ of meaning. Imagination, producing new metaphors or revivifying old, is not the cause of truth, but its condition."[9] Perhaps those secret pictures are expressions of imagination, the organ endowed to us by our Creator with which we infuse our grief with meaning.

Even as I type, I find it difficult to express how precious my secret pictures of my dad have been and how they've illuminated my understanding of his life's value. Perhaps my difficulty lies in the fact that his value is ineffable in and of itself. Data-fying his life could result in an equally ineffable loss.

In fact, it might be worse if an AI simulation gets our loved ones right all the time. If pattern recognition coupled with voice and video sampling are enough to simulate a person, that could communicate that people are just patterns of data. Consciousness is much more than that, as we've already seen. But for future generations that increasingly see the world in terms of data and its manipulation, will reality have collapsed for them such that they come to see human beings as little more than patterns and algorithms? Will death—and the life it punctuates—lose depth of meaning? Will it come to be seen as artificial as the software that simulates it?

I'm not advocating against using such AI applications. What I'm advocating is that we anchor ourselves to reality as we ride the AI waves that come. Because AI-Mania doesn't just amuse us by creating artificial worlds. AI-Mania artificializes the world.

Machines to Save Our Lives—Machines Dehumanize

The cultural schizophrenia with which we live causes us to vacillate between self-love and self-loathing, between exaltation and humiliation. We marvel at our ingenuity but resent our limitations. We are awed by the brain's complexity but reduce it to an undesigned product of mindless nature. We welcome AI as our human-created savior, and yet we fear that AI is the harbinger of our obsolescence.

If we are the product of mindless evolution, then "human intelligence is not the special characteristic we think it is," claims Cambridge University scientist Venki Ramakrishnan. Yet he also says, "We humans define our very existence by our ability to think. So it is not surprising that, in an anthropomorphic way, our fears about AI reflect this belief that our intelligence is what makes us special."[10] Put another way, we are not special because we are not designed. Yet we design machines that can surpass us, making them special (instead of us). When an AI is named *Time* magazine's Person of the Year, perhaps we'll feel the dehumanizing sting as acutely as many women felt it when *Glamour* magazine named Caitlyn Jenner among the 2015 Women of the Year.[11]

For the transhumanist, it's only a matter of time before AI surpasses human beings, so the only way to maintain our value (or even just survive) is to merge with it. *If you can't beat 'em, join 'em.* Rothblatt believes mindware can liberate us from our bodily limitations, and Elise Bohan longs to be freed from what she calls our "ape-brained meat sacks."[12] The AI-Manic disdain for our bodies is curious, is it not?

The transhumanist hope is not limited to perpetuating a recording of our thoughts after death, but it also includes the merging of our consciousnesses with the Singularity so we'll never die. As we've already seen, given the immateriality of our consciousness and the eventual heat death of all storage media, this is wishful thinking. Uploading data and patterns isn't uploading a person. The fullness of what it means to be human isn't merely computational capacity; it involves immaterial awareness, feeling, and sensation.

While not identical to our bodies, awareness, feeling, and sensation are intertwined causally with our bodies. Any state of being devoid of them would not be post-human in a progressive sense, but *inhuman* in a regressive sense. Your hormones and nerve endings convey feeling that your mind interprets as sensations. Your mental states flood your body with such emotion that your eyes leak with tears. Your joys exhilarate you. Being surprised elevates your adrenaline. We are meant to be a functional unity of mind and body.

After the Singularity merger, however, when our minds no longer interact with our so-called meat sacks, even the memory of what it was like for our minds and bodies to be linked will fade, degraded to mere phantom sensations. Imagine being free of your meat sack. We will become more computational and less empathic and empathetic. Our interactions will become transactional, like supercomputers in a network.

While some people, even some theologians, consider such a merger to be the coming kingdom of heaven, Meghan O'Gieblyn is less optimistic. Sensing that our algorithm-enforced homogeneity is merging us into a hive mentality and "that the soul is little more than a data set," she says, "I don't know exactly what to call this state of affairs, but it does not feel like the Kingdom of God."[13]

The Future Is Now

We need not wait for dystopian science fiction to see that transhumanistic AI-Mania has overhyped our silicon salvation. In his book *I, Human*, business and consumer psychologist Tomas Chamorro-Premuzic finds that no matter how advanced technology gets, it only seems to heighten our worst proclivities. "The most notable thing about AI is ... its ability to exacerbate certain human behaviors, turning them into undesirable or problematic tendencies," he writes. "Irrespective of the pace of technological advancement, and how rapidly machines may be acquiring something akin to intelligence," he continues, "we are as a species exhibiting some of our least desirable character traits, even according to our own low standards." Chamorro-Premuzic critically warns, "This aspect of the AI age ought to concern us most: this is not about automating humans, but degenerating or deteriorating humanity."[14] Like me, Chamorro-Premuzic doesn't believe we ought to abandon using AI or developing it further. That would be neither realistic nor prudent. But also like me, he recognizes that a silicon savior is no savior at all.

Moreover, AI-Mania is making us less authentic, collapsing the reality of what it means to be human with and into the reality of what it means to be a robot. "Although AI has been rightly labeled a prediction machine, the most striking aspect of the AI age is that it is turning us humans into predictable machines," according to Chamorro-Premuzic. And AI "has reduced the variety, richness, and range of our psychological experience to a rather limited repertoire of seemingly mindless, dull, and repetitive activities."[15]

Those mindless, dull, and repetitive activities we give in to so easily stem from unthinkingly affirming the algorithms' suggestions about which video to watch next, whether to buy a pasta maker, and what cuisine to try tonight. Is it any wonder, then, that Oxford's 2024 Word of the Year was "brain rot"?

The technology is not to blame. Our desire to relinquish our agency to it is. "We appear to have surrendered our humanity to the algorithms, like a digital version of Stockholm syndrome," writes Chamorro-Premuzic.[16] Perhaps the greatest reality collapse of all is the subtlest: the way we've allowed distractive technology to fool us into believing that life outside our devices is the distraction. The more addicted to our devices we become, the more prone we are to ignore life. Chamorro-Premuzic writes that "it is arguably more appropriate to see life as the actual distraction, since, statistically speaking, it has been downgraded to an occasional psychological interruption from our nearly perpetual state of digital focus and flow."[17]

Think of what we communicate when we think of our bodies as ape-brained meat sacks. Our bodies become incidental to humanness. In the time between now and our technological liberation, we—especially young people—begin to hate our bodies. All of us, to varying degrees, are dissatisfied with our bodies, but young people need little prodding to feel deep insecurities about how they look and feel. Social media already offers them an escape from reality by allowing them to favor and promote a digitally altered appearance. Calling our bodies ape-brained meat sacks that we can shed in favor of an improved digital version renders the body a mere shell.

We once invented machines to stand in for us and save us from body-damaging toil, like harvesting crops and lifting iron girders. I think back to *Her* and Samantha's failed attempt at intimacy with Theodore, where the machine uses a human woman as a marionette. Theodore was right to feel unsettled, because the body, while not the same as the mind, is linked to it and therefore is not a commodity or mere vessel. Transhumanism reduces our bodies to mere sacks of meat. The Bible calls our bodies temples of the living God (see 1 Cor. 6:19). The chasm between the two is galactic.

Transhumanism and Faith in the Myth of Progress

Michael Burdett, a philosopher and scientist, argues that the transhumanist expression of AI-Mania rests on what he calls the "myth of progress," which claims that "the present is a diminished form of what is to come. It is not complete, but rather often signals the discrepancy between the imperfect present and the fulfilled and perfect future."[18] Burdett isn't using *myth* in the sense of a false belief or belief without evidence. Rather, he's using *myth* in the classical sense of an idea or story that inspires wonder and meaning, irrespective of its objective truth. According to Burdett, we assume that time plus ingenuity equals progress. We glance back at our technological advances and see the elimination of child labor, the minimizing of workplace accidents, and breakthroughs in medicine. Such progress is a blessing, to be sure.

But moral setbacks have waltzed with the progress. We've invented vaccines and antibiotics but also chemical and biological weapons. We've invented nuclear power plants along with nuclear bombs. In fact, Nick Bostrom, one of transhumanism's prominent advocates, believes that humanity is unlikely to go extinct from a natural calamity like an asteroid strike or a super-virus. Instead, he thinks we're more likely to go extinct through the abuse of technology, like weapons of mass destruction. Yet (and apparently without irony) Bostrom simultaneously believes that human technological advancements will save us from extinction.

At the risk of seeming too lowbrow, I can't help but think of the episode of *The Simpsons* in which the fictional town of Springfield is thrown into an uproar when alcohol is banned. When the ban is repealed, the townsfolk drunkenly celebrate, at which point Homer Simpson makes a toast. "To alcohol: the cause of, and solution to, all of life's problems!"[19] Hoping in human ingenuity to save us from the very human ingenuity that threatens our existence is quintessentially a belief in myth.

Transhumanism, as an expression of AI-Mania, is dangerously naïve about human nature. If, as O'Gieblyn noted, all existential questions have become engineering problems, transhumanism reduces the complexity of human sin to behavioral quirks that simply need tuning. As such, transhumanism has no framework with which to warn against the dangers to come—not dangers brought about by AI, but by the human misuse of AI.

AI-Mania's Unbalanced Equation

It isn't much of a leap to go from a transhumanist view of humanity to a mechanistic one that equates humans and machines. But balancing the equation entails canceling out our humanity.

As software systems mimic human-level intelligence more accurately, some ask whether we'll be able to tell when, if ever, machines become self-conscious such that they have rights we are morally or legally obligated to protect. Nick Bostrom tackles the question from the perspective of conscious suffering. He rightly notes that conscious suffering—what philosophers call *second-order suffering*—is qualitatively different from experiencing pain, or *first-order suffering*. Lower creatures experience first-order suffering. Think of a spider that loses a leg. It doesn't despair about the loss; rather its nerve clusters just register the pain. Conscious or second-order suffering occurs when a creature not only feels the pain but experiences emotional, moral, and existential distress *about* the suffering. Higher animals, like deer or even chimps, might feel emotional distress about their pain, but they don't ask existential questions like, "Why me?" And as far as we can tell, suffering about suffering is uniquely human. That aboutness, as we've already seen, is a mental state very different from a brain state, implying that consciousness is immaterial, not biological or mechanical.

Bostrom brushes past that implication when he wonders whether purely physical AI systems will experience second-order suffering, necessitating that we limit AI research or halt it altogether.[20] George Church, a professor of Health Sciences and Technology at Harvard asks, "How do we know that a sociopath, a coma patient, a person with Williams syndrome, or a baby has the same free will or self-consciousness as our own?"[21] Even though we don't know the answer for certain, we still afford them rights. So, Church further asks, should we extend rights to computer systems that mimic human behavior, even if just at the infant level?

Church claims that the more we study human consciousness so that we can emulate it in computers, the more machinelike the brain appears to be. No matter how machinelike the brain is, however, it is not the seat of consciousness. And so when Church mistakenly equates consciousness with the brain, it's unsurprising that he concludes that humans and machines could become morally coequal.

Consciousness is based on more than gray matter and computational power. The uniqueness of our consciousness points to an indelible quality unique to humanity, something very much like the biblical concept of the *imago Dei*. And perhaps trying to equate AI systems with human consciousness is a form of collapsed reality in which we anthropomorphize machines and de-anthropomorphize people.

As she thoughtfully wrestles with the line distinguishing human from machine, O'Gieblyn notes that we use computational metaphors for humans and human metaphors for machines. We alternatively say things like, "The brain performs so many calculations per second," and "My computer is going crazy." Are we thereby signaling to ourselves that consciousness doesn't make humans special?

"Rodney Brooks, the MIT roboticist, insists that [consciousness] confers on us, as humans, a distinction we no longer warrant," O'Gieblyn writes. "In his book *Flesh and Machines*, he claims that most people tend to 'overanthropomorphize [sic] humans ... who are after all mere machines.'"[22] That's a jarring statement with wide implications that we dare not gloss over because, historically speaking, over-humanizing people hasn't been our problem. And if Chamorro-Premuzic is right, we're using technology to dehumanize each other ever more.

Brooks likely isn't advocating indifference to our fellow humans. But his view is materialism's logical outworking, and it exposes transhumanistic AI-Mania's fatal flaw in trying to resolve the humans-are-machines-and-gods contradiction. Its solution is, in the final analysis, artificial. It focuses entirely on invention and equates invention with progress. We'll invent things because we can. And because we can, we have an obligation to. We'll worry about the consequences and morality later. Sure, eggs will be broken, but just think of the omelet we're making! Our specialness as humans is no longer warranted because we're nothing more than machines. That doesn't sound like progress, no matter how many flashing lights we put on a metal box or how fast our laptops are.

Pagan Romans were not guilty of over-anthropomorphizing humans but undervaluing them. Gladiators were forced to die for a mob's amusement because to the Romans those men's lives had no purpose but entertainment. When we think of each other as mere utilities, we regress to the worst of our worst history. As John Gray writes, "Enterprises such as transhumanism and the technological conquest of death are the inevitable end-point of liberalism once it is has been wrenched from the matrix of theology in which it originated. Unbounded self-determination, however, is a fantasy. Human beings cannot create their lives out of nothing, but they can destroy the life they have and be left with nothing."[23]

AI-Mania won't result in unbounded self-determination, just unbounded drab existence. AI-Mania sees us as machines with neither designer nor design. AI systems, though designed, will still lack ultimate or objective purpose and meaning, which will render even our merger with them meaningless. Absent such purpose, AI-Mania solves the contradiction by destroying the life we have, leaving us with nothing but perpetual existence.

With erudition, O'Gieblyn guides us through part of her loss of faith in the Christian God, pointing to what she believes is meaningless suffering in the Old Testament book of Job. There, Job is described as a righteous man who praises God and serves him. Satan challenges God, saying that if God takes away all that Job has, even his family and his health, Job will curse God to his face. God takes Satan up on the challenge and allows Satan to inflict massive suffering on Job.

Job, in his second-order suffering, asks existential questions about why God has allowed this to happen. God doesn't answer Job's questions. Instead, God asks Job questions meant to help Job understand that he is in no position to question the Almighty. And Job is satisfied, because his encounter with God satisfies a deeper need than any answers could. When Job acquiesces after encountering God's dizzying presence, God restores Job's health, family, and fortune.

O'Gieblyn's objection is that God, who seems to know everything and can do anything, chooses to conceal his motivations and methods from Job. In other words, God hides the purpose of Job's suffering from him. Though Job is restored to health and prosperity, O'Gieblyn feels that he is left with the trauma of not knowing why he went through it all. Job is a book of the Bible that I've read a lot since my dad's murder. My previous view, that the book is laced with deep meaning surrounding suffering and purpose, has been solidified as I continue to wade through the waters of my grief.

What O'Gieblyn's loss of faith and my increased faith share is a thirst for meaning and purpose. Though we've come to different conclusions about God, I'm grateful that in her book about artificial intelligence, she places meaning and purpose front and center. Meaning and purpose, and the quest to find them, make the most sense in a God-created world. This hints that the answer to our cultural schizophrenia is to be found there.

The public discourse over AI's development has fallen into two prevailing camps, colloquially called the *boomers* and the *doomers*. The boomers see AI as almost entirely good and promising, and therefore they want to see its progress boom. The doomers see AI as almost entirely bad and apocalyptic and want a moratorium on its development. My analysis here may give the impression that I am a doomer. I can assure you that isn't so. I'm quite a technophile and look forward to responsible AI development and implementation. I *am* a doomer, however, about AI-Mania and transhumanism, because they offer no solution to the cultural schizophrenia.

Interestingly, in a chapter about the ways in which AI is making us more impulsive, Chamorro-Premuzic ends with a section entitled "Is There Hope?" There, he concludes that self-control, which he says tires like a muscle, is needed to counter the trend toward becoming shallower versions of humanity. I agree that this is part of the solution. Yet despite all his insightful and incisive analysis, his solution to our self-control problem is essentially the kind of advice one can find in a health magazine: Get more sleep and exercise.[24] As he points out, we—not the technology—are the problem. Yet he endorses our ability to control ourselves as the solution.

To effectively and consistently exercise such control, transcendence is needed—transcendent purpose and transcendent assistance for that which ails us. The Bible counts self-control as a fruit not of our flesh or human will but of the Spirit of God (Gal. 5:22–23). No matter how many spiritual-sounding words are thrown into AI-Mania's mix, it ultimately mechanizes human beings and thus has no hope of solving the humans-are-machines-and-gods contradiction. There is no avoiding the question of purpose and meaning. If any solution is worth embracing, it must be one that is objectively meaningful and purposeful. Otherwise, why do it? Because it is devoid of such purpose, AI-Mania's cure for our cultural schizophrenia is worse than the malady.

There is another view that offers a solution. But it isn't Bioclasm.

Chapter Seven

FROM THE TOP DOWN: BIOCLASM'S PSYCHOLOGICAL SIDESTEP

Unlike AI-Mania's bottom-up approach to cultural schizophrenia, Bioclasm—as defined in our exploration of reality collapse in chapter 1—approaches the contradiction from the opposite direction. Rather than claiming that we're machines that can engineer our way to godhood, it positions us as already divine sovereigns whose preferences should override material reality.

John Gray captures this dynamic when he writes, "The hyper-liberal project is to emancipate human beings from identities that have been inherited from the past. Human beings must be free to make of themselves whatever they wish. The result is an artificial state of nature among self-defined identities."[1] An "artificial state of nature" is Gray's artful way to say that our efforts to forge identities outside the realm of nature create a contradiction. Artificial things are not naturally occurring things, after all. And so Bioclasm hasn't solved the machines-and-gods contradiction, only reformulated it.

Without Self-Deification, What Are We?

Bioclasm's self-making cure brings neither peace nor respite, because it's not offered—it is imposed. Burton notes that self-making has a storied history that includes tales of those who have gone from rags to riches and obscurity to social media celebrity. But according to Burton, we have come to the point where self-making determines our personal worth. "[I]f we do not manage to determine our own destiny, it means that we have failed in one of the most fundamental ways possible. We have failed at what it means to be human in the first place."[2]

As we suffer through our cultural schizophrenia, we have to be our own psychiatrists, and we can only prescribe self-making, obstacles like biology be damned. We've obligated ourselves to be not merely humans but self-creating humans. The power to self-make is a divine quality, which means that for Bioclasm, to be human is to be divine. Now, Burton is addressing a broad cultural phenomenon, not identity ideology per se. But judging others as less than fully human for failing to self-create logically follows from Bioclasm, especially as it pertains to gender.

Since Caitlyn Jenner appeared on the cover of *Vanity Fair* in 2015, the number of people, mainly young people, identifying as transgender has skyrocketed, with young females identifying as transgender or seeking a female-to-male transition showing a startlingly steep increase.[3] According to data published by Reuters just from one clinic, the Doernbecher Children's Hospital in Portland, the number of patients given gender-affirming care went from sixteen in 2013 to 724 by 2021.[4] In the past decade, the admissions to gender-reassignment clinics have mushroomed by 4,000 percent.[5]

As social psychologist Jonathan Haidt remarks, at least two factors account for some of the increase. First, the population of transgender people used to be based on adults electing to have gender-reassignment surgery (an obviously low number) but is now determined from a broader population. Second, the stigma that surrounds gender non-conformity has relaxed, encouraging more people to publicly identify as transgender.[6] While these factors surely account for a small increase, it strains credulity to think that they account for such astronomical surges.

Haidt, who lauds increased acceptance of transgenderism as social progress, believes that the increase is due at least in part to social influences, especially among Gen Z girls:

> The recent growth in diagnosis of gender dysphoria may also be related in part to social media trends.... But the fact that gender dysphoria now often appears in social clusters (such as a group of close friends), the fact that parents and those who transitioned back to their natal sex identify social media as a major source of information encouragement, and the fact that gender dysphoria is now being diagnosed among

> many adolescents who showed no signs of it as children all indicate that social influence and sociogenic transmission may be at work as well.[7]

Some have castigated Haidt for promoting a right wing, fringe theory about transgenderism. Labeling him as right wing dismisses the growing research (that has been suppressed) about the theoretical phenomenon called *rapid-onset gender dysphoria* (ROGD). ROGD theorists note that clusters of young people, especially girls in middle school and high school who showed no prior signs of gender confusion, experience explosive growth in trans-identification after one of their peers publicly identifies as trans. According to research conducted by Lisa Littman of Brown University School of Public Health, 87 percent of adolescents with ROGD either have friends who announced themselves as gender dysphoric, or had saturated themselves with material from niche websites discussing gender dysphoria, or both.[8]

Positing a sociogenic cause for dramatic psychosocial phenomena among adolescents is not novel to ROGD, which means it isn't an easily dismissible fringe theory. Suicide contagion, for example, is the well-documented phenomenon in which suicidal ideation and attempts rise amongst adolescents after one of their peers attempts or commits suicide, especially if media coverage brings attention to the tragedy.[9] Even the suggestion of suicide can lead to an increase. The *Journal of the American Medical Association—Psychiatry* reported a 28.9 percent increase in youth suicides in the month after Netflix released the show *13 Reasons Why*, which dramatized a fictional teen girl's rationale for ending her life.[10]

Haidt cites other examples of sociogenic psychological phenomena, such as when scores of young people who follow social media influencers who have Tourette's syndrome or dissociative identity disorder (DID, formerly called *multiple personality disorder*) mistakenly believe they have Tourette's or DID.[11] Is it so far-fetched, then, to theorize that a similar phenomenon could be happening with young people and gender confusion?

Bioclasm creates a milieu that valorizes a student who comes out as transgender. Indeed, regardless of one's views on transgenderism, a young person's public declaration can be an act of courage. But it can easily influence her peers to respond to the culturally imposed obligation to self-make by identifying as trans, despite a prior lack of true gender confusion.

As a natural part of puberty, adolescents struggle through the anxieties that come from social complexities and budding sexual awareness. Bioclasm injects social steroids into already anxious minds, fostering gender confusion where it didn't exist. Identification as transgender might momentarily elevate a young person from merely human to social deity, but it ultimately fails both those suffering from genuine dysphoria and those who have been coaxed into thinking they do. The aura of self-making might emanate from the attention (positive or negative) the first girl receives, thus encouraging her peers to similarly self-make. All of them are hoping that doing so will finally qualify them as human.

Detransitioner Chloe Cole describes the elation she felt while being valorized during her transition, only to find it fleeting.[12] As Cole learned the hard way, self-making as a cure for cultural schizophrenia can be more than a mere detour on the path to self-discovery. Bioclasm exerts social pressures on young people and their parents to stay on the path of self-making through gender nonconformity.

As we've already seen, adults, especially parents, are pressured to affirm and encourage chemical and surgical transitions for young people. To do otherwise is a hateful oppression of a child's sovereignty that will, they say, inevitably lead to the child's suicide. But as we've also seen, suicidality isn't inevitable if a person doesn't transition—unless we continually communicate that suicide is the only alternative to transition.

And transitioning may itself foster suicidal ideation. Testifying before Congress, Chloe Cole commented that she felt suicidal only *after* surgery to remove her breasts. "My parents almost got the dead daughter promised to them by my doctors. My doctors had almost created the very nightmare they said they were trying to avoid."[13]

Bioclasm's consequences reach beyond the lives of those with gender dysphoria, of course. But self-making requires that we ignore the over six hundred women athletes who have been robbed of 890 medals by biological men who bested them at women's sports by March 2024.[14] We must ignore the women who have been raped and abused in prisons by male inmates who transferred from men's prisons merely by identifying as women and without undergoing any screening for lying.

And never mind the stories of people like David Reimer and Nathan Verhelst, both of whom transitioned for different reasons but killed themselves when they couldn't reconcile the contradictions their lives had become after transition.[15] We must ignore—and even silence—the voices of detransitioners like Chloe Cole, Kyla Gillespie, and Laura Perry, all of whom have endured excruciating physical and psychological pain from transitioning from female to male. Self-making isn't optional—it's compulsory.

Everyone agrees that gender dysphoria is not a mental state any of us should exist in. There are two ways to care for those whose mental perception of their gender doesn't line up with their biological sex. One is to focus on changing the body. Another is to work on changing the mind. Bioclasm endows the mind with divine autonomy, so we must focus on getting the body to conform to our mental will. Thus, Bioclasm is just a reheated version of ancient Gnosticism—the view that the physical world is a prison from which our spirits must escape. The body becomes the source of all that's "wrong" with the person—an obstacle our infallible preferences must overcome.

Scan here for Kyla Gillespie's detransition story

This may seem like a spiritually and psychologically authentic cure because it encourages human agency. But it's actually artificial. Focusing on the body masks the underlying psychological issues and trauma that usually cause so many to experience dysphoria. We do them no favors when we ignore that which is truly hurting them. How ironic that we consider self-making fundamental to being human, only to discover that it too often leads to self-destruction. Is it really so surprising to discover that artificial self-making has natural consequences? Those well-documented consequences have led more and more governments to pause or halt the prescription of puberty blockers to minors, even with parental consent.[16]

Unchecked, Bioclasm's tsunami can still surge ahead, washing over the tragedies by cleverly following a new path that avoids the pitfalls of physical transition altogether. For example, Van Ethan Levy—a self-described "queer, non binary, trans, Egyptian, Jewish, Latine, autistic individual with dynamic disabilities and many more excluded identities"[17]—wrote an article entitled "Why the Term Transition Is Transphobic" for Therapy Route. Levy argues that transition is transphobic because "[w]e are and always have been our gender.... [C] hanging how we look on the outside is not a transition."[18] Helen Joyce responds, "For such activists, medical or surgical transition is simply a matter of choice for those trans people for whom it seems meaningful. Altering the body is no part of attaining a new identity, but if the body is a mere meat puppet, why not alter it if you wish?"[19]

That really is the logical outworking of Bioclasm because its foundation is our autonomy. Biology can be altered, but it doesn't have to be. This cleverly dodges the counterpoint that altering biology to fit our desires tacitly admits that the body limits our divinity. But Bioclasm shuns such an admission. Where AI-Mania has to reduce us to machines, Bioclasm makes our machines our playthings.

That's the heart of Levy's claim that transition is transphobic. To solve the humans-are-machines-and-gods contradiction, Levy essentially elevates us to godhood. That does nothing, however, to alleviate the underlying psychological comorbidities. In fact, Levy's solution is worse than physical transition because it exalts the underlying anxiety, bipolar disorder, depression, and dysphoria to divine virtues. And so they go untreated, perhaps even intensified.

A Cure That Worsens the Disease

The consequences to our bodies and minds expose our so-called sovereignty to be utterly artificial. Both vaginoplasty (creating a vagina out of male sex organ tissue) and phalloplasty (creating a penis out of female sex organ tissue) require not only lengthy, painful recoveries but also lifelong maintenance.

A person who has undergone a vaginoplasty must commit to a lifelong dilation routine, which involves dilating the "neovagina" multiple times a day to prevent it from closing. The body never accepts the neovagina as a legitimate organ but reacts to it as a wound in perpetual need of healing. In the case of phalloplasty, functional difficulties require fistulas and implants that need maintenance and replacement. In both cases, infections are a constant risk. And in both cases, patients need lifelong hormone therapy to maintain secondary sex characteristics as their bodies continually try to return to the state in which they were born.

Add to this the fact that dysphoria and suicidality persist after transition, and any illusion that transition is natural dissipates like vapor. These are the consequences of living in the artificial state of nature Gray warns us about. Future medical techniques may prevent the ongoing medical horrors of transition. But such a destination—if it exists—is far away. The road to it will be paved with human suffering.

I can't help but think of Carlo Collodi's 1883 children's story, *The Adventures of Pinocchio*. Collodi's original story (before Disney adapted it) was about a wooden puppet that repeatedly gets into trouble through mischief, deceit, laziness, and keeping bad company. Pinocchio becomes enfleshed when he takes care of his ailing father, Geppetto, having learned what it means to be selfless, responsible, and forthright.

In other words, Pinocchio became real—who and what he was meant to be—because he conformed his identity to reality: in this case, moral reality. The story presupposes the existence of objective moral values and the objective duty to act in accordance with that truth. Because morality is a property of persons, transcendently objective morality exists only if it is grounded in a transcendent person. And a transcendent person, of course, describes God quite well.

So long as Pinocchio tried to bend moral reality to his will, he remained artificial, a contrivance. But the artificial boy becomes genuine, authentic, and truly alive when his desires conform to the objective reality around him. We, too, will remain inauthentic, ever trapped in the angst of our schizophrenia, if we hold on to the myth that our identities are as malleable as steel. Our sense of autonomy is like Icarus's wings—they carry us aloft on the jet streams but elevate us higher than we are entitled to go. We will share Icarus's fate and fall hard when reality's heat melts our waxy contrivances. Those who continue to struggle with gender dysphoria well after transition and have to fight their bodies' natural inclinations for the rest of their lives aren't as godlike as Bioclasm promised them they'd be.

Bioclasm's Artificial Additives

Listening to the voices of detransitioners and why they experienced dysphoria in the first place exposes Bioclasm's artificiality. They did not transition because they were born with an innate sense that their bodies were the wrong sex. No, many developed dysphoria and eventually tried to transition only after they came to dread or even despise what it means to be their natural sex. Negative social messages about their natural gender combined with their mental health struggles, giving birth to that dread and loathing.

For a long time now, men have been derided in popular culture as less intelligent, less moral, and more aggressive than women. Think, for example, of television shows and movies portraying fathers as well-meaning but dim-witted goofs whose wives and children have to fix the messes they've made of things. When men aren't depicted as Homer Simpson, they're characterized as abusive fathers or husbands. There are very few examples in popular culture of morally upright, socially responsible, and nurturing men. They have to be superheroes to be virtuous. And even then, they are narcissistic or troubled men trying to be superheroes.

Sociologists have written bestsellers that depict natural male behavior as precursors to misanthropy and misogyny, labeling it as the beginning stages of toxic masculinity. Every man, if we listen to pop culture and sociology, is a ticking time bomb. I admit that this is speculative, but perhaps some men develop gender dysphoria because they first develop misandry. The only way to escape their imposed self-loathing is to remake themselves into what the culture considers a more moral, intelligent, and thoughtful being.

There is evidence, though anecdotal, that something similar is happening to young women who develop gender dysphoria. In a recent interview, detransitioner Chloe Cole told me that her dysphoria started in her prepubescent years when she became uncomfortable with her developing body and the attention she got because of it. She dreaded menstruation, feared the pain of pregnancy and giving birth, and believed that she would be perpetually vulnerable to assault as a woman.

Such thoughts are natural, but when they began to interfere with her everyday life, a therapist suggested to her and her parents that she might be transgender. From there, Chloe's natural insecurities and anxiety as a twelve-year-old girl developed into gender dysphoria and ultimately an attempt at transition that she thought would free her. But it didn't. After four years in which she lost her breasts to surgery, suffered the effects of cross-sex hormones, and became suicidal, Chloe stopped her transition. Today, she recognizes that she is, has always been, and will only ever be a woman. Her involvement with the growing community of detransitioners brought her in contact with men and women who relayed similar stories of how they felt not so much that they were the opposite sex as much as they dreaded or hated the sex they were born into (scan QR code left).

Scan here to find out what led to Chloe Cole's feelings of dysphoria

What all of this indicates is that gender dysphoria, while a real psychological affliction, isn't the root issue to be addressed. Focusing solely on dysphoria or gender transitioning in some form obscures the reality of what so many are going through and leads us down paths of unhelpful—even harmful—treatments.

What tells us that this is the case? After a person's transition, his or her underlying psychological problems remain or worsen. Suicidal ideation persists or worsens. So many injections of chemicals foreign to the body are needed to maintain the transition that the person's body forever rebels against. Reality—in this case, biological reality—protests louder than any rally ever could. And its protests are not in the public square; they are in the bodies and lives of dear people who are being convinced that there are five lights when there are only four.

When the Two Shall Meet

We are just biochemical machines, one voice tells us, but we can aspire to become godlike machines when we merge with our artificially intelligent offspring. We are gods, another voice proclaims, who can bend our mechanistic biology to suit our preferences.

These are the views offered by AI-Mania and Bioclasm, respectively. Both surged from the post-truth seaquake in opposite directions, with AI-Mania emphasizing our technology and Bioclasm emphasizing our divinity. Our lust for autonomy propels both tsunamis powerfully enough to traverse the whole world and converge. Only the dam called *reality* stands in the way. As the tsunamis converge on reality from two sides, it seems as if the answer to the humans-are-machines-and-gods conundrum is intoxicatingly close. Spiritual-sounding words like *technium* and the *Singularity* beguile us into thinking that reality can be whatever we make it.

Tech entrepreneur Martine Rothblatt, a biological man who identifies as a woman, sees AI-Mania and Bioclasm's twin quests for human autonomy converging in our near future. The title to Rothblatt's 2011 self-published book, *From Transgender to Transhuman: A Manifesto on the Freedom of Form*, declares that position quite clearly. Helen Joyce, an atheist who presumably doesn't believe that humans have immaterial souls, nevertheless recognizes that despite the lofty goal of human exaltation, Rothblatt's aim of mixing technology and identity reduces humans to machines: "If [Rothblatt's book] seems reductionist, consider Bina48, a robot Rothblatt commissioned in 2007. A disembodied head with thirty motors under its rubber skin that allows it to make expressions, it was modeled on Bina Rothblatt, the woman Martine married as a young man and has remained married to since transitioning in 1994, and was trained to respond and converse using recordings of her."[20]

Here, we have gender dysphoria culminating in an AI companion for a transitioned person. This is but one example of how the two tsunamis are converging.

Now, if Rothblatt is right that transhumanism is the logical extension of gender-identity ideology, and if transhumanism offers only an artificial solution to our cultural schizophrenia, then it follows that Bioclasm's cure is just as artificial—and just as deficient. Mathematically, multiplying two negatives equals a positive. In life, however, combining two artificial ideologies doesn't result in authenticity. In their efforts to exalt humanity to divinity, AI-Mania and Bioclasm reduce us to triviality.

Perhaps the cure for self-doubt is not self-deification. Perhaps the cure is found not in trying to reconcile the irreconcilable but in seeing humanity as something more than machine yet less than divine. Perhaps the real cure is found not in reducing the body to a mechanism that can be upgraded to godhood nor in exalting ourselves to be gods trapped in meat puppets subject to our whims.

Perhaps when we see our bodies as temples of the transcendent and our consciousness as a reflection of our Creator's image, we can find the cure.

Chapter Eight

DIGITAL EDEN

The Syllogism

As we delve into the question of who that Creator is and if he exists, a syllogism will scaffold my main argument. My claim is that the biblical God exists, that he created us in his image, and that he imparted a message to us—through the Bible and Jesus—that guides us reliably through the waters of identity and technology, in contrast to the confusion of AI-Mania and Bioclasm.

The syllogism has the following structure:

1. If an ancient book consistently describes and predicts the human condition with unmatched accuracy over the centuries, it is more likely to have a source beyond human insight.
2. The Bible has consistently described and predicted the human condition with unmatched accuracy over the centuries.

3. Therefore, the Bible is more likely to have a source beyond human insight.

I realize, of course, that other thought traditions—like Greek philosophy, Confucianism, Buddhism, Hinduism, and Islam—also offer insights about pride, corruption, identity, and meaning. But what I hope to show is that biblical wisdom about these areas of existence stands apart in its uncanny depth, consistency, thoughtfulness, and redemptive power.

The Bible spoke to the ancients to whom it was written, and it speaks to us today. Lesslie Newbigin called Jesus "our eternal contemporary."[1] The Bible, which points to Jesus, qualifies for that same status. Its transcendent wisdom serves as the sextant navigating us past the cultural tsunamis rushing toward the dam of reality. Perhaps we can outpace them and fortify the dam with mortar that binds the bricks of our identity with the bricks of God's identity, interlocking the two to provide our ultimate purpose.

Predicting Our Quest for Godhood

"This isn't going to stop.... A.I. won. Humans lost." That's not a quote from *The Matrix*, *The Terminator*, *Ex Machina*, or the myriad films warning us that reckless reliance on artificial intelligence will lead to robot overlords. Jason Allen, the contestant we met in chapter 1 who won first prize in an art contest using Midjourney, spoke those words. He uttered them in response to criticism that he had cheated by using AI and that what he submitted—while beautiful—wasn't art. "Art is dead, dude. It's over. A.I. won. Humans lost."[2]

Allen's story struck me because I dabble in digital art using my iPad. His response to the criticism did more than pique my interest;

it unsettled me. *Such odd comments coming from an artist,* I thought. *Art is dead. It's over. AI won. Humans lost.* Allen wasn't defending his victory; he was gloating over humanity's defeat at the hands of its own creation. It's as if he forgot that he is human and not AI.

Pondering further, I realized that Allen's boast wasn't really that odd. It was human, profoundly human. His boast was paradoxical, to be sure, reflecting the cultural schizophrenia with which we are afflicted. Allen's boast seemed to be a declaration of human defeat. But fundamentally it was a boast that human ingenuity had created something superior to humanity itself—even in art, which sets our species apart. It is human nature to boast about our achievements, especially when they exalt us to hitherto unreached heights. And with AI's victory in that art contest, Allen boasted about humanity's victory—not against AI nor against itself but against God. We've been dying to gloat like that almost since humanity arrived on the scene.

In Genesis, we read that God placed Adam and Eve in the paradise of Eden, commanding them to enjoy its fruits and tend to it, thereby coupling pleasure with purpose (Gen. 2:5–25). God endowed them with authority over creation and freedom to eat from any tree in the garden except one. "[O]f the tree of the knowledge of good and evil you shall not eat," God commanded, "for in the day that you eat of it you shall surely die" (v. 17). Carefully note the wording of God's command.

Trouble enters Eden in the form of the serpent, who tries to lure humanity away from our very purpose, which is communion with God.[3] The serpent craftily misquotes God, asking Eve, "Did God actually say, 'You shall not eat of *any* tree in the garden'?" (Gen. 3:1). Of course, God said no such thing. He gifted them with the fruits of every tree but one. Eve catches the misquotation but responds with her own.

"We may eat of the fruit of the trees in the garden," she begins, "but God said, 'You shall not eat of the fruit of the tree that is in the midst of the garden, *neither shall you touch it*, lest you die'" (vv. 2–3).

God never prohibited Adam and Eve from touching the fruit of the tree of the knowledge of good and evil. He commanded only that they not eat it (Gen. 2:15–17). When Eve misquotes God's command—possibly a misquotation that Adam had told her previously—humanity reveals its craving for autonomy over freedom, for sovereignty over communion with God. We exposed our vulnerable underbelly.

Seeking our doom, the serpent collapses reality by twisting our weakness into an opportunity for strength. "You will not surely die," the serpent whispers. "For God knows that when you eat of it your eyes will be opened, *and you will be like God*, knowing good and evil" (Gen. 3:4–5). The serpent suggests that God had withheld knowledge from humanity, knowledge we are entitled to possess. But God did not withhold knowledge of the good. Adam and Eve had known and experienced good all their lives. While it was true that their eyes would be opened upon eating the fruit, they also would behold evil for the first time. Adam and Eve were created innocent, not perfect. And in their imperfection, they would be unable to resist the serpent's wiles.

Before that moment, Adam and Eve had abided by God's command to refrain from eating the fruit of that tree, communing with God who often walked with them "in the cool of the day" (see v. 8). They were satisfied with their God-given authority over the rest of creation. But once they believed the lie that the fruit would elevate them to being God's rival, they forsook it all. The fruit would ultimately feed more than their desire for knowledge. It would also feed their desire to transcend their creaturely status and attain divine power. And so, they ate and plunged the world into decay (vv. 6–7).

Lest we judge Adam and Eve too harshly, let us not forget that our desire for godlike autonomy has never waned. Today's post-truth obsession with autonomy over freedom is the contemporary expression of the age-old human tendency to value power over purpose, and it has touched and influenced us all. AI-Mania is one modern form of that age-old temptation. Bioclasm, which turns the immaterial soul into a malleable identity, is another. Jason Allen's paradoxical boasting about technology that will surpass us included a telling observation about human nature: "The ethics isn't in the technology," he commented, "*it's in the people.*"[4] He's quite right. AI itself isn't evil. In fact, it has the potential for marvelous benefits and in many ways is delivering on that potential. Neither is self-discovery evil. But our human penchant to forsake ethics when faced with the possibility of aggrandizing ourselves is the problem.

This is a problem the Bible anticipated centuries ago. That Scripture describes our tendency so accurately lends credibility to that ancient tome's historicity and wisdom. The same vulnerability in the human heart that we see throughout the Bible remains wide open today to AI-Mania and Bioclasm's serpentine whispers.

We build machines capable of feats that exceed human ability, then we boast about how they surpass us. We write algorithms that analyze patterns and make decisions faster than human brains can process, and then we follow the algorithm's advice. We design neural networks that mimic artistic creativity, then award prizes to the simulacra we've forged. Sherry Turkle warns that "technology is seductive" because it "meets our human vulnerabilities."[5] Our vulnerability isn't that we want to create machines to make our lives easier. It's that we find the possibility of erasing Eden's failure intoxicating. In our post-truth eyes, Eden's failure was not that we rebelled against God, but that we rebelled too soon, before we were equipped to achieve transcendence.

Technology and social engineering, so we think, have finally given us what we need to beat God at his own game of creation, by doing something that even the almighty God cannot do: create a god equal to or greater than himself. Classical monotheism holds that while God can do the naturally impossible, like create and interfere with the laws of nature to perform miracles, he cannot do that which is unreasonable and inconsistent with his nature. For example, God cannot create square circles. Circles, by definition, don't have corners, whereas squares, by definition, have corners. Creating a square circle would be to plunge the ordered world into a state of utter disorder because it renders logic arbitrary. Performing miracles is not the same thing because miracles don't suspend logic, just the laws of nature at a given moment.[6]

Since God is the foundation of logic, reason, and order, doing something logically absurd would violate his very nature. He would, in that sense, cease to be God. Similarly, it would be absurd for God to create another perfect being. Why? Because a perfect being would not need a creator. And since it's logically absurd to create an uncreated being, God cannot create a being just like himself, and certainly not one greater than himself. Through AI, however, humanity thinks itself to be on the precipice of power that eludes even God.

The way we refer to our new technology implies that we believe it to be the apotheosis of human achievement. We call it *artificial intelligence.* It's a broad and romanticized term that includes large language models, deep learning algorithms, and generative software, most of which have limited capabilities.[7] They are not, as we've already seen, *intelligent*. The software can perform calculations, absorb volumes of material, and generate output at speeds far exceeding human capabilities. But the abilities to receive input, identify patterns, and simulate language aren't true intelligence because, as Searle showed, they don't equate to understanding. True intelligence from a true mind entails so much more, including the ability to think abstractly, consider counterfactuals, and produce output born of imagination and inspiration.

AI leaders like Yoshua Bengio and Stuart Russell acknowledge that the current technologies don't do any of this. Sure, they might be good at chess, Go, and other games, but playing a game and pondering the problems of chemistry are worlds apart.[8] Despite AI's current limitations and lack of, well, intelligence, we still call it artificial *intelligence*.

Calling the technology we currently have something that it's not (and may never be) allows us to imagine that we've birthed a godlike being. This is its own form of reality collapse. Kurzweil's response when asked if there is a God was, "Not yet," after all. With the Singularity's impending advent, we finally will have bitten the fruit once denied us but without, they say, the effects of Edenic exile. We will have succeeded at what God could not even attempt.

Yuval Noah Harari has noted that AI's development might lead to a future where AI-generated religious texts will capture the devotion of humanity. "Religions throughout history claimed a nonhuman source for their holy books," he writes. "[S]oon that might be a reality. Attractive and powerful religions might emerge whose scriptures are composed by AI."[9] The irony is hard to miss. Humanity, in its drive to rival and even surpass God, will create synthetic gods instead. Human beings are incurably religious, which forces us to worship something, even things we create. This merely repeats the idolatry of old, an idolatry whereby we forsook the earth's Creator in favor of earthen idols we created.[10]

Ironically, the Bible, the ancient wisdom we try to replace with our techno-idols, anticipated our idolatry with piercing insight. "Claiming to be wise, they became fools, and exchanged the glory of the immortal God for images resembling mortal man and birds and animals and creeping things" (Rom. 1:22–23). The harm, however, isn't merely that our idolatry offends God, but also that it robs us of the sublimity God intends for us.

Imitation Becomes the Highest Form of Battery

Our misguided quest for autonomy extends beyond AI-Mania to include Bioclasm's rejection of the created order, especially the gender binary that undergirds our species' existence. By positioning itself within broader social justice movements, Bioclasm gains moral urgency while obscuring its fundamental contradiction. We have a legitimate moral imperative to act with compassion and understanding toward the infinitely precious people suffering from gender dysphoria. Beneath Bioclasm's disguise, however, lurks a motive ulterior to seeking mind-body congruence. Bioclasm seeks to uproot the created order and re-landscape Eden with a tree whose fruit allows Adam to become Eve or perhaps a mixture of the two.

Bioclasm does this with little regard for the damage done to those who suffer from gender dysphoria. That much seems evident from the fact that the science supporting gender-affirming care is so weak and the science suggesting its harm is so strong—and suppressed.

In a startling *New York Times* op-ed entitled "My New Vagina Won't Make Me Happy," transgender activist Andrea Chu admits that "until the day I die, my body will regard the vagina as a wound." Chu confesses that "I am a marshland of regret.... I was not suicidal before hormones. Now I often am." For Chu, not even surgery has removed the shame and self-loathing. And yet Chu's op-ed still advocated for the surgery that has brought such misery.[11]

The Bible chronicles human efforts at achieving transcendence through emergent technologies or social trends. Genesis 11:1–9 recounts that humanity settles in the plains of Shinar, rejecting God's command to spread out over the earth. Gathered there, they construct a ziggurat—a step-pyramid with a shrine for a deity at its apex. The tower's height is unprecedented in ancient times and represents a technological and social attempt to achieve human sovereignty. "Come, let us build ourselves a city and a tower with its top in the heavens, and *let us make a name for ourselves*, lest we be dispersed," the builders say (Gen. 11:4).

This plan goes against God's intentions to create diversity that will be unified not by human pride and sinfulness, but by God's grace and love. Observing the construction, God determines to confuse their language because "this is only the beginning of what they will do. And nothing that they propose to do will now be impossible for them" (v. 6b). God's concern is that humanity's capacity for harming itself through pseudo self-deification will spiral out of control.

God isn't trying to shackle human progress through imposed ignorance. In fact, the Bible reveals that the tower of Babel story doesn't portray a God who divides our language to maintain a narcissistic form of dominance. Centuries after Babel, during Pentecost, God reveals a unifying gospel message of hope to diverse people through their native tongues by miraculously causing them to understand each other (Acts 2:5–13). On the plains of Shinar, God confuses language to preserve diversity and prevent human folly. On the day of Pentecost, God unites human diversity to express his plan to restore all people to our authentic selves.

Yet we resist such blessings to our detriment. We do things that we know may harm us because deep down, humans are gamblers. Of course, we have to take some risks, otherwise progress would be impossible. Adam and Eve were gamblers too, but the stakes were incredibly high. They weighed God's warning of impending death should they eat the forbidden fruit against the serpent's promise that they would become like God if they ate it. One can view that gamble in two ways. Rationally speaking, if eating the fruit entailed even the slightest possibility for humanity's doom, no possible benefit would be worth the risk. Passionately speaking, however, even the slightest possibility that the serpent was right made the reward seem like it was worth the risk.

We made the irrational choice then and are doing so still. The Bible's insight into human nature explains why the AI developers whom *New York Times* columnist Ezra Klein interviewed felt an obligation to continue their work despite knowing that it presented a possibility of disaster. While there wasn't uniform agreement, Klein felt it fair to say that most of the developers felt an obligation to "usher in" the new form of intelligence. That wording struck author Paul Kingsnorth as religious in its tone.[12] Ushering in what? Perhaps the Singularity, perhaps the technium, but no doubt something that would look like a god of our creation.

I can't help but recall my conversation on the airplane with the software executive from chapter 1. She lamented that we had plunged into social media without knowing what it would do to us (though as we'll see below, Meta, then Facebook, apparently had a strong hunch), only to find ourselves in a worse social state. In the same way, we are rushing into AI and gender-affirming care without knowing what they will do to us, even though we have Haidt's evidence and the science revealing gender-affirming care's detriments. Yet still we rush in. Distrusting God's warning that the forbidden fruit would upend their utopia, Adam and Eve thought they knew what eating from the tree of the knowledge of good and evil would do to them.

We are not as removed from Eden or Babel as the centuries of our progress would have us think. Our manic (and sometimes coerced) immersion into technology doesn't produce human authenticity; it *masks* authenticity and takes us farther from what was originally intended. For example, Frances Haugen, a former project manager for Facebook (now Meta), testified before the US Senate in October 2021 that Facebook deliberately designed its platform to maximize user engagement—even at the expense of users' mental health.[13] She testified that Meta intentionally optimized its algorithms to promote content that sparked strong emotional reactions, including anger and outrage, because that's what keeps users engaged longer.

In his book on the effects that AI is having on humanity, Chamorro-Premuzic recognizes that the issue lies with human nature, not the technology itself. After pointing out that Twitter (now X) users quickly trained Microsoft's chatbot to use foul language and post racist and sexist tweets, Chamorro-Premuzic quipped, "[N]o prizes for guessing where the dark side was engendered, that is, human versus artificial intelligence. The fact that humans get a kick out of making chatbots do antisocial, sexist, racist things clearly says little about AI's dark side and a great deal about the dark side of human psychology."[14]

Of course, we need to implement good policies and employ useful technology to curb bad behavior and reward good behavior. But without a deeper—I daresay *biblical*—understanding of why we act the way we do and what the spiritual solution is, we are doomed to failure.

"The heart is deceitful above all things, and desperately sick; who can understand it?" God says through the prophet Jeremiah (Jer. 17:9). From the lips of Jesus, we learn, "For out of the heart come evil thoughts, murder, adultery, sexual immorality, theft, false witness, slander" (Matt. 15:19). As we wrestle with this condition, we find that the apostle Paul spoke for all of us when he wrote, "I have the desire to do what is right, but not the ability to carry it out. For I do not do the good I want, but the evil I do not want is what I keep on doing" (Rom. 7:18–19). Perhaps unwittingly agreeing with Paul, Chamorro-Premuzic laments that, "If kindness were a given, a default reaction, then we wouldn't be spending so much time lamenting that we don't have enough of it, or encouraging more people to be kind."[15]

The fact that AI-Mania and Bioclasm seek our "improvement" through technology and bespoke identities implies that they both recognize something is flawed with humanity. As Mary Harrington puts it, "Over the twentieth century, a consensus seems to have emerged that the problem with modernity was not the paradigm itself; rather, the weak point in the project of utopian masters was *us*."[16] The world we experience mirrors the world we'd expect if the Bible accurately describes the human heart. Many of today's thinkers merely echo the Bible's thirty-five-hundred-year-old insights.

Yet some of their solutions ignore the wisdom found in that eternally contemporary text. They ignore the personal change that flows from spiritual redemption, which is a necessary condition for social change. They propose to improve our technology or come up with ways to relabel our identities, which only isolate us or mollify us, respectively.

In *The Abolition of Man*, C. S. Lewis points out that when a society discards the moral wisdom of history, it doesn't create a better morality but only new forms of oppression based on the whims of the socially dominant. And when we try to master the moral fabric of the world, we become slaves to our impulses and our creations.[17] When we try to master reality through technology and outside the bounds of objective morality, we become slaves.

Using technology like shovels, plows, hay balers, and personal computers allows us to subdue nature in accordance with God's will (see Gen. 1:28). The problem comes when we employ technology to supplant God's will. We want to master God, so we create AI. Yet AI doesn't rescue us from the sin that lurks within. It exacerbates that sin because we jettison biblical insight. We employ AI as a way to traffic human beings by creating deepfakes of real people and selling them, commodifying each other (and ourselves), and ceding our decisions to algorithms.

Similarly, we try to master God through self-created identities, redefining the binary that makes humanity possible in the first place. But we find ourselves in need of constant injections and medical procedures because our biology refuses to be mastered. Even after the injections and procedures that were meant to bring clarity, the minds of those with gender dysphoria stumble in the fog of continued confusion and thoughts of suicide.

Other worldviews, whether religious or secular, provide at least partial diagnoses of the human condition in various forms. As comparative religions professor Stephen Prothero puts it, "What the world's religions share is not so much a finish line as a starting point. And where they begin is with this simple observation: something is wrong with the world."[18] Despite underlying differences, the finish lines for secular humanism, Islam, and pantheism have a commonality: Human beings can earn, and at some level deserve, an ultimate reward—be it heaven, moksha, enlightenment, or a better society and longer lifespans. According to secular humanists, humanity determines ethics and can educate itself to utopia.

Interestingly, Elise Bohan, an author and senior research scholar at Oxford's Future of Humanity Institute, admits that humanity's problem is humanity itself, which means that we have only one place to go: up. But Bohan doesn't mean we look to God; she means we work toward a better, more tech-infused version of ourselves. She writes, "[H]umanity will be hard pressed to make it through this century alive if we do not invent technologies that render us less susceptible to short-term thinking, cognitive biases, tribalism and human stupidity."[19] But short-term thinking and cognitively biased, tribal, and stupid humans will be the very people who will supposedly invent our savior-tech.

Pantheists, for their part, hold that through proper thoughts, deeds, and meditation, we can work out our karma and achieve enlightenment. Confucians cling to the belief that we can improve and perfect ourselves.[20] And though Islam teaches that attaining heaven is subject to God's mercy, we can earn that mercy when our good works outweigh our bad deeds (Sura 7:8–9).

I submit that all these solutions are merely variations on a theme of human self-help. They recognize that the problem is us, but they rely on us to fix the problem. The Bible, however, digs deeper by describing our problem not as behavioral but foundational. The Bible stands apart by logically placing the solution outside of us and onto the redemptive work of God.

We will get to the heart of that solution in short order. For now, it suffices to say that the Bible uncannily predicts that whether through religion, technology, or social change, human beings avoid God-reliant solutions in favor of remedies that involve self-reliance. To that end, it's interesting that Chamorro-Premuzic and others correctly call AI a "prediction machine."[21] It turns out that we've had a prediction machine of sorts in the form of Holy Writ, describing and predicting human nature long before any of our modern intellectuals were born.

Neither Prisons nor Playthings

Human-centric solutions that don't take human sin seriously have a way of rejecting the essence of what it means to be human. Consider Rothblatt—the brilliant entrepreneur, transhumanist, and transgender activist—who envisions a not-so-distant future where we can upload our consciousnesses to digital "mind clones."[22] Our mind clones would exist in "lives" parallel to ours. When we biological creatures "expire," our mind clones can persist in near perpetuity, unencumbered by the finitude of biology or the strictures of gender. Of course, the mind clones would not contain our actual consciousnesses and thus not give us immortality. So why would anyone want to create a mind clone of themselves?

Because, according to Rothblatt, we can each have a best friend who is identical to us. We can work out our issues, solve problems, and even disagree with our mind clones. Naturally, one wonders how our mind clones can be useful if they're mere copies of us and we're just biochemical machines programmed to behave and believe a certain way. But that isn't really the point, you see. The real point is not to have a robot buddy in this life but to create a robot race to populate the world.

This is similar to the goals advanced by Bohan in her book, *Future Superhuman: Our Transhuman Lives in a Make-or-Break Century*, where she predicts a possible future in which we create a new species to succeed us. We will create not only a god through AI, but also a race to be its high priests.

Rothblatt describes the mind clone project as a kind of liberation—a means of overcoming the limitations of biology. As a living embodiment of the nexus between AI-Mania and Bioclasm, Rothblatt argues that gender is not tethered to biology. Bohan argues that technology will free women from childbirth. Sex and gender, then, are entirely matters of self-definition. We are not bound by the bodies we were given; we are self-created beings. At the 2015 SXSW conference, Rothblatt cautioned that while some regulation is necessary, "[w]e can never get to a point where we, like, make it illegal for people in hacker space to create novel forms of consciousness."[23]

Just as AI promises liberation from mental limitations and transhumanism promises liberation from physical constraints, so Bioclasm promises liberation from social boundaries. The created order—whether biological, mental, or spiritual—is seen not as redeemable. Rather, Bioclasm and AI-Mania see the material world, especially the human body, as either a plaything or a prison, respectively. For those like Rothblatt, who straddle Bioclasm and AI-Mania, our bodies are both.

It turns out, however, that neither Rothblatt's nor Bohan's ideas are all that novel. They are the techno version of humanity's centuries-old quest for immortality. In fact, they borrow heavily from the biblical idea of a physical and eternal resurrection of the faithful; they just jettison God from the process. Such visions, indeed the immortality quest of all transhumanists, pay the backhanded compliment that the Bible's vision of humanity's future is worth taking seriously. The Bible seems to emerge whenever we seek to drown it in the tides of our ambitions.

And so, among the Bioclasts and transhumanists, there remains an ambivalence about human essence. "Techno-utopians," writes theologian Jacob Shatzer, "insist on essential definitions of things like 'intelligence,' but they resist any essential definition of 'human' or 'person,' because the whole transhumanist project is built on exceeding and improving everything, which resists the idea of preserving any 'essence.'"[24] And if we cannot define what is essentially human, how can we define what is essentially male or female? Bioclasm rejects the idea that either sex or gender are essential parts of human existence. If one can identify as the sex opposite of what their body dictates or can claim a gender that is neither male nor female (such as gender fluid or agendered), then the terms *male*, *female*, *man*, and *woman* have no essential meaning.

While I emphasize that gender dysphoria is a genuine psychological phenomenon, I've often wondered how someone who claims to be a woman trapped in a man's body can know what it's like to be the opposite sex. Sure, a biological male may express himself more femininely than other men, just as a biological woman may express herself more masculinely, but he wouldn't actually know what being a woman truly feels like, nor would she know what being a man is actually like.

For example, Thomas Nagel posited a thought experiment about what it would be like to be a bat. We know how bats behave. We can predict how they react in certain circumstances. But we'll never know what it's like to be a bat because our essence isn't chiropteran.[25] And while I know what it's like to be a male child because I once was one, I'll never really know what it's like to be a female child. I can't know the insecurities that attend being a young girl who is starting puberty and worried about her first menstrual cycle. Such a thing is completely foreign to me, both mentally and physically, due in no small part to the fact that I lack the female hormones and sex organs that influence a girl's mental states as she matures. Neither my body nor my mind were designed for such experiences.

Yes, my daughters have described to me (with plenty of hesitation) their coming of age. I can only approximate an understanding of what they've gone thorough by analogy to my own teen years. But I will never know what it is to *be* a maturing female who worries about biological functions and how they affect social life and daily living. For a biological male to claim otherwise is the height of hubris and gender stereotyping, which is why Dylan Mulvaney's celebration of "girlhood" strikes so many women as offensive.[26]

The understanding of my essential differentiation from my daughters has helped me become adept at reading the look my wife, Nicole, gives me, communicating that a particular shedding of my daughter's tears will not be alleviated by male intervention. Having competed in athletics for most of my life, I know how males react to competition and loss and how male teammates interact and work out conflict. Having watched my girls compete in athletics, I can safely say I don't fully understand women's athletic psychology. I have some idea, but I will never know what it's like to be a woman on a sports team.

I don't know what it is to essentially be a female because I lack female *essence*. By contrast, I deeply know what it's like to grow up as a male dealing with the hormones that rage inside when double-digit years approach and cloud my judgment and frustrate my confidence. I experienced the awkwardness of having my body do something utterly involuntary at the exact wrong social moment. I know how male dynamics work in social and competitive situations. I can guide my son through his phases of life because I know what it's like to be him *essentially*.

So, when someone says that they are a woman trapped in a man's body, it seems to only express an approximation of womanhood based on observations of outward appearances and gender stereotypes—the very stereotypes we tend to shun.[27] A man cannot know womanhood in any objective sense, nor can a woman understand manhood. So we have to ignore gender essentialism or redefine it as *feeling* like the opposite sex or gender, or no gender at all. As Katie McCoy puts it, "[T]he expression of gender is regarded as the essence of gender."[28] But this is simply question-begging, isn't it?

Our bodies are neither prisons nor playthings, but sacred vessels that can follow a current toward a redemption in which we remain human, not post-human, and yet not merely physical. The Christian hope is that the bodies of those who embrace the gospel message will be resurrected in a glorified physical state. Our physical bodies will interact with the world in new, as-yet-unimagined ways. Jesus was raised physically, yet his glorified body could walk through a locked door behind which his disciples skulked, fearful of the authorities who had just crucified Jesus (see John 20). He showed them the vestigial crucifixion scars as proof of his physical form, which imparted hope and peace to even the staunchest skeptic in the room.

The Hebrew word for *glory* literally means "*weighty*," causing C. S. Lewis to remark that Jesus' glorified body could walk through the locked door because, compared to him, the locked door was but a vapor.[29] As Jesus was our representative on the cross, dying in our place, Jesus is the exemplar of our bodily resurrection, where our bodies will be so weighty that the world will not be the obstacle it is today (1 Cor. 15:42–49).

So much for the popular caricatures of heaven, where we float as disembodied beings playing harps amidst the clouds. For the Christian, the material world is not something to be denied or escaped but redeemed and renewed. "All this materiality is to be embraced rather than denied," writes Stephen Witmer. "The goal of the Bible is not to free a pure spirit from tainted flesh but to affirm the inescapable mutuality and the unity of body and spirit, and teach how they might exist harmoniously."[30]

Transhumanist AI-Mania sees the body as a prison one must escape by melding with technology. At best, the data of our brains will be uploaded to a physical storage medium. We will not be immortal; only our data will be, and that data will be housed in something physical (and therefore ultimately doomed to heat death). The transhumanist merely exchanges a fleshy prison for a silicon one, all in the name of self-assertion over the divine.

Similarly, the Bioclast sees the body as both a prison and a plaything for anyone wishing to alter their anatomy and chemistry to conform to their psychological state. Yet as Andrea Chu, Chloe Cole, and Kyla Gillespie testify, healing remains elusive following transition. For most people with gender dysphoria, the prison remains—only its plumbing has been changed. The words of the prophet Jeremiah come to mind: "They have healed the wound of my people lightly, saying, 'Peace, peace,' when there is no peace" (Jer. 6:14).

The Bible speaks to the war between the body and the spirit. While it is hotly debated whether the apostle Paul was speaking of the spiritual struggles of unbelievers or believers, it remains the case that the Bible recognizes that humanity struggles with a dysphoria between what the mind wants and what the flesh demands (see Rom. 7:18–25).

Empathizing with those who so struggle, Paul writes, "I myself serve the law of God with my mind, but with my flesh I serve the law of sin" (v. 25). He rhetorically asks, "Wretched man that I am! Who will deliver me from this body of death?" (v. 24). He reveals the answer but a moment later, an answer that has nothing to do with software engineering or social engineering. The answer is personal because the answer is a person, the engineer of our souls. "For the law of the Spirit of life has set you free in Christ Jesus from the law of sin and death" (Rom. 8:2). Paul goes on to explain that the cross, where Jesus paid the collective penalty incurred by Adam and Eve and perpetuated by us all, reconciled us spiritually to God, even though our bodies groan with the rest of physical creation until its coming renewal (vv. 3–4, 22–23).

One may retort that if after embracing Christ the anguish of the dysphoria remains, why not embrace AI-Mania or Bioclasm as solutions? The answer is that following Christ risks none of the mental and physical anguish that Andrea Chu, Chloe Cole, and so many others have experienced. Further surgeries and hormone treatments provide no comfort. In fact, they bring the opposite. But Jesus provides comfort and hope, even as our pain persists. No stranger to discomfort and pain, Paul was able to endure it by relying on the "God of all comfort, who comforts us in all our affliction, so that we may be able to comfort those who are in any affliction, with the comfort with which we ourselves are comforted by God" (2 Cor. 1:3b–4).

Scan this QR code to watch my debate with atheist author John Loftus on the evidence for Jesus' resurrection

Referring to our bodies as tents, Paul wrote, "For while we are still in this tent, we groan, being burdened...." But comfort is coming in that God will renew the bodies that cause us anguish and beckon death, "so that what is mortal may be swallowed up by life" (2 Cor. 5:4). The reason to embrace that comfort—the comfort that the suffering-acquainted Paul embraced—is Jesus' bodily resurrection, which precedes and makes possible our own.[31]

The Blessings of Belly Buttons

As we navel-gaze over our efforts to define ourselves and improve upon humanity, we miss out on what our belly buttons reveal about who we are and who God is. The navels we gaze at (but seldom truly contemplate) are ever-present reminders of our *dependency*—at least upon our mothers. Stanley Hauerwas and William Willimon put it pithily:

"Nothing is quite as ontologically revealing as our belly button. It's our body's way of reminding us that we are not self-made people, we are not separate islands, we are not merely rugged individuals."[32]

Transhumanism seeks to shed that dependency through a post-human state, but it can never truly achieve full autonomy because we will always be subject to physical laws and the reality of what came before us. Post-humans will simply have a new umbilicus that ties us to a machine of some kind. Even on a purely materialistic framework of reality, we are reliant on the energy that keeps molecules in motion—energy we can neither destroy nor create—but energy that will be disbursed across the closed system of the universe, resulting in its entropy-death.

Bioclasm's attempt at autonomy is more ideological than technological but no less flawed. Inventing new gender monikers, changing our dress, or altering our bodies tacitly acknowledges a preexisting foundation. We didn't create that foundation, so we can never be truly self-made, only altered. The Bioclastic belly button is not technological but philosophical.

Whether transhumanist or Bioclastic, there's no escaping dependency. Ironically, all our efforts at self-making turn out to be navel-gazing. Creating new umbilici that tether us to our technological or ideological creations doesn't liberate us from being reliant on God for our being.

Gottfried Wilhelm Leibniz's *argument from contingency* makes a simple but profound point: Everything in the universe is contingent—it exists, but it didn't have to. And because contingent things don't have to exist, their existences cry out for an explanation. My existence is contingent on a host of prior explanations, like my parents, the circumstances of their meeting, my parents' parents, and so on. Even the universe is contingent. It came into being according to the standard cosmological model. And even if it were eternal, the universe could have been smaller or larger, with more or less mass or energy.

But if every contingent thing depends on another contingent thing for its existence, we end up with an infinite string of prior explanations and events that never actually explain anything. If the chain of past causal events were infinite, we could never start the chain to count up to the moment that is now, the moment you're reading this sentence. And so there must be something that isn't contingent—a *necessary being* whose existence explains itself—to start the chain of causal contingent events.[33]

Of course, as contingent beings ourselves, we have difficulty comprehending a being with no beginning or prior cause. But as Leibniz shows, a necessary being must exist as a matter of logic. The only viable candidate to fill the office of necessary being is a powerful, eternal being. And given the exquisite fine-tuning of the universe for life's existence and the exquisitely specified complexity of that life, it appears that the necessary being made choices to bring us about. All considered, the necessary being Leibniz argued for looks a lot like God.

But Leibniz helps us see only that an all-powerful, conscious God is the source of our existence. We need more specificity if we are to understand who that God is and what our relationship to him is.

Neither the gods of the Greeks nor the gods of the Babylonians nor the deities of any non-Abrahamic faith will do. Those gods, by their very creation accounts, are contingent beings. The Titans created Zeus and the Olympian deities. The Titans themselves were born from the primordial deities Gaia, Eros, and Uranus. And they emerged from Chaos, which isn't a deity but the void from which everything emerged.

The same holds true for the Mesopotamian gods like Marduk and Tiamat. Such gods are poor candidates for the necessary being Leibniz showed must exist.

The Bible, however, not only describes God as a necessary being but also weaves the sophistication of a cosmological argument—one that Leibniz articulates centuries later—into its description of God. Exodus 3 recounts Moses' famous encounter with God in the burning bush that is not consumed (Ex. 3:1–14). During that encounter, God reveals his name to Moses as "I AM that I AM" (v. 14 NET). In doing so, God gives Moses more than a title or label. Leibniz argued that there must be a necessary being, a self-existent being from which all contingent beings are caused. God's revealed name is not just a statement of existence but declaration of his self-existence.

He doesn't merely exist. He is existence itself. He is the foundation of reality, quite unlike and utterly superior to the gods of pagan pantheons. Lest we think that the divine moniker smacks of pantheism or even panpsychism, we need only read the personal interaction that *I AM* has with Moses to see that he isn't the impersonal creative force of the universe. We need only read God's declaration in Exodus 3:6 that "I am the God of your father, the God of Abraham, the God of Isaac, and the God of Jacob" to see that God is not one with the universe; he is distinct from it though intimately concerned with it and the humans who inhabit it.

It has always struck me as particularly poetic that in light of the linguistic marvel he's just heard, Moses doubts his ability to carry out God's mission due to his own lack of eloquence. Yet God assures Moses that the right words will come at the right time (Ex. 4:10–12). God's revealed name is not just a demonstration of linguistic elegance and efficiency but also of philosophical and theological brilliance. What philosophers like Leibniz labored to articulate in complex terms and syllogisms, the Lord of language encapsulates in but a single word: Yahweh—*I AM.*

Leibniz's point cuts through the illusion of self-sufficiency and the myth of self-creation propagated by transhumanistic AI-Mania and Bioclasm. No matter how advanced our machines become or how many self-definitions we contrive, they'll always be contingent—because we too are contingent. Our creativity, intelligence, and even our existence depend on something beyond ourselves. We may create machines that outthink us or social paradigms that relabel us, but we'll never create something that explains its own existence. That belongs to God alone.

Of course, C. S. Lewis poetically expresses our dependence on God for our very being. "The suns and lamps in pictures seem to shine only because real suns or lamps shine on them; that is, they seem to shine a great deal because they really shine a little in reflecting their archetypes."[34] We shine because we reflect the image of the One who creates all things.

But what God has ordained for humanity in general and each one of us in particular exceeds whatever machinations and schemes we have for ourselves, something we'll explore soon. Seeing God's purpose in our creation provides the guidance we need to navigate new and exciting technologies that benefit us all without succumbing to the fantasies and foibles of AI-Mania. Embracing the identities he has for humanity and for each human lights our paths—as painful as they may be for those of us struggling with self-understanding.

Our contemporary return to Eden's temptation flies in the face of not only philosophy but also prophecy. The biblical story of Eden is both an account of humanity's fall and a warning about what happens when contingent beings scoff at logic and the reality of the necessary authority from which we sprang. In this fact alone, that the biblical account of Eden and even the very name of Eden's God subsume a sophisticated philosophical argument for God's existence and our dependence on him, we see evidence of the Bible's divine authority. Having that authority, it can reliably guide our self-understanding.

No Improvement or Revision Necessary

The serpent in Eden convinced Adam and Eve that they should be more than what they were created to be. As Kelly Kapic puts it, the serpent implies "that divinely given limits are a fault to be overcome rather than a beneficial gift to be honored."[35] The seeds of transhumanism and Bioclasm were thus already planted in the primordial garden. But the transhumanist's rejection of our bodies and brains as "ape-brained meat sacks" insults what God intended us to be. Transhumanists are like Cavil, the Cylon who is frustrated by the limitations of his human likeness (see chapter 4). Likewise, the Bioclastic rejection of the natural human binary scoffs at God's design.

Yet the fact that the limitless second person of the Trinity incarnated himself opposes such ideas. Incarnation—literally, *enfleshment*—expresses that the physical body is inherently good, despite our corruption of it. To rescue it from that corruption, God expresses the humility of "taking the form of a servant, being born in the likeness of men" (Phil. 2:7). As Kapic notes, "The doctrine that the Word became flesh means that God himself affirms our flesh as good, and that affirmation liberates us from apologizing for our creaturely limitations."[36]

God the Son is eternally incarnate in the body of Jesus, which is and ever will be physical and also glorified in the state the human body was meant to be. Paige Comstock Cunningham makes the point that "in creation, we see a God who pronounces that the world is good, and that humankind is very good, not in need of revision."[37] Indeed, I agree. Humankind is not in need of revision—just redemption.

Chapter Nine

AI-KIDO

A Lesson about Leverage

I trained in various martial arts from grade school into my late twenties, culminating in mixed martial arts. With my six-foot-eight-inch frame, keeping opponents outside their striking range but within mine was my secret to success. But grappling was another matter. When I dabbled in aikido—a Japanese martial art involving only throws, twists, and joint locks—my first few classes were quite the lessons in the effectiveness and power of leveraging another person's momentum against them.

I had been paired with a more experienced student for a basic maneuver called *irimi nage*. I wasn't sure he could pull off the technique on me—I towered over him by at least ten inches and outweighed him by eighty pounds. When he saw that I knew how to move and maintain balance, we shifted into a speedier phase. I launched my attack with considerable speed, confident my size and strength would overwhelm any technique my opponent might hope to use. I suddenly felt the room spinning vertically and found myself on my back in an arm bar.

Aikido means "the way of harmony with energy," and a practitioner blends with his attacker's motion, redirecting the force rather than opposing it directly. My partner had done exactly that, leveraging my size, strength, and speed against me to his advantage.

Pointing to the Ultimate Mind

With AI-Mania's rise, assumptions about whether human intelligence makes us unique—and whether our intelligence implies a transcendent creator—spar with counter-assumptions that we are merely "ape-brained meat sacks" that emerged through blind evolutionary forces. Consider, for example, comments from Nobel laureate Venki Ramakrishnan. He acknowledges that we don't understand consciousness or even how we do things as simple as remembering phone numbers. He paraphrases former Google chairman Eric Schmidt, who said that designing a robot that could clear a dinner table, wash dishes, and put them away was enormously challenging.

As Ramakrishnan admits, the human brain "can do all these and also do mathematics and music, and invent games like chess and Go, not just play them. We tend to underestimate the complexity and creativity of the human brain and how amazingly general it is."[1] Despite his astonishment at the brain's complexity and consciousness's enduring mystery, Ramakrishnan asserts that human intelligence doesn't set us apart qualitatively from other animals or even AI, since all are products of evolution. "Human intelligence is not the special characteristic we think it is," he says, "but just another survival mechanism not unlike our digestive and immune systems, both of which are also amazingly complex."[2]

His statement fails to account for vast differences between humans and, say, alpacas—both of which have digestive and immune systems, but only one of which knows that spitting on others is rude. Nevertheless, in lockstep with the naturalistic evolution, Ramakrishnan reduces intelligence to a survival mechanism: "Intelligence evolved because it allowed us to make sense of the world around us, to plan ahead, and thus to cope with all sorts of unexpected things in order to survive."[3] But his statement, that "[i]ntelligence evolved because it helps us make sense of the world," is a tautology: conscious intelligence isn't a tool for sense-making—it *is* sense-making. His claim is like saying the ability to make sense of the world evolved because it's useful for making sense of the world.

Naturalistic evolution puts brilliant thinkers like Ramakrishnan in the odd position of admitting that our minds haven't grasped how they work while insisting that our minds arose from mindless accidents. But artificial intelligence hasn't arisen by mindless accident. Brilliant minds fueled the enterprise, suggesting that our intelligence needed an even greater mind to design it.

Stoked by reductive naturalism, AI-Mania lunges forward, overconfident of its strength, only to discover that theism has leveraged AI's momentum to put AI-Mania on its back. What seems incontrovertible is that AI hasn't emerged from the ether. The computer hardware that houses the algorithm-processing silicon chips were designed by someone. The algorithms themselves were designed; they didn't arise by chance or by random bits of code cobbling themselves together in a digital primordial soup.

As *Merriam-Webster* tells us, something is artificial if it is "made, produced, or done by humans especially to seem like something natural."[4] Human minds have worked intentionally for decades to create artificial intelligence, with disappointing failures and surprising successes. Now we've created something remarkable in its capabilities yet still a far cry from having human-level intelligence. Recall Gopnik's sobering comment that AI hasn't risen to the learning capabilities of the average four-year-old. The implication seems clear: If it takes this much human intelligence to create something that cannot yet rival a child, it must have taken an intelligence far beyond our imagination to create that child's mind.

What about AI seeming to learn independently? Some models programmed to translate French into English have started learning Italian without being programmed to do so. Is this unintended intellectual evolution? If so, could our intelligence also have evolved without intention? It's highly unlikely. Even when algorithms veer into unprogrammed areas, they stay within their general programmed parameters. An LLM might learn languages beyond its original programming, but LLMs don't spontaneously dive into string theory or interior design.

This distinguishes AI from human intelligence and consciousness. We don't just process information from our environment along limited parameters—current learning machines do that through preplanned data sets. We, on the other hand, observe our world and wonder if we can make something new. We postulate about creating things that don't exist. *We imagine. We invent.* AI does not.

Judea Pearl, director of UCLA's Cognitive Systems Laboratory, notes the slow computer learning process resembles the eons-long way evolution is theorized to have developed superb vision in eagles and snakes. But, he says, that process cannot explain "the super-evolutionary process that enabled humans to build eyeglasses and telescopes over barely a thousand years."[5] Pearl calls our counterfactual imagination "super-evolutionary," a label that supposedly replaces a supernatural explanation. But, as Raymond Tallis and Thomas Nagel argue, our imaginative faculties defy evolutionary explanation. If evolution took millions of years just to develop sharp vision in animals, how much longer should it have taken to develop a brain capable of improving its own vision through creative imagination? It simply hasn't had enough time.

AI doesn't create—it generates. Allen's Midjourney-generated art contest submission wasn't art. Fascinatingly, when Allen filed for copyright protection, claiming he was losing money from others' unlicensed use of his submission, the US Copyright Office denied him because his submission *lacked human authorship*.[6] Ironically, the Copyright Office determined Allen's art is dead. Doubly ironic is the fact that several artists are suing Midjourney for stealing their artwork to train the AI platform that created Allen's submission.[7]

When we try to collapse reality, reality resists. Creativity involves counterfactual imagination that Midjourney lacks. It requires looking at a blank canvas and imagining what could enliven the white space—feeling that it shouldn't be left blank. Human creativity involves qualitatively different prompts than Midjourney obeys. While Midjourney must be told what picture to (admittedly impressively) cobble together based on works human artists have previously created, the dance of light across a lake at sunset awes a human artist into painting a novel interpretation of it. AI can simulate creativity but cannot experience it.

According to Chamorro-Premuzic, our capacities have led cognitive science researcher Margaret Boden to believe that "the human mind is a great deal richer, more complex, and subtle than we originally assumed, at least when the AI field got started."[8] That our minds are so much richer than the AI we painstakingly created suggests that our minds are the handiwork of an infinitely greater mind. At an October 2023 conference, I watched MIT AI developer Rosalind Picard discuss how AI has impacted her faith in Christ. Her answer was simple but profound: "I am in even more awe of the ultimate mind."

Inventor Stephen Wolfram, however, tries to erase the distinction that awes Picard, claiming that it is simply "another part of the Copernican story: We used to think Earth was the center of the universe. Now we think we're special because we have intelligence and nothing else does. I'm afraid the bad news is that that isn't a distinction."[9]

Wolfram imagines a future in which human consciousness can be uploaded and virtualized in a computer storage medium—"a box of a trillion souls." Inside, Wolfram says, "there will be molecular computing going on ... all kinds of elaborate stuff." Next to this box sits a rock with its own "elaborate stuff going on" at the subatomic level. The only difference is the box's elaborate stuff is based on the long history of civilization and memory. The rock has its own history—a geological one.

Thus, according to Wolfram, there's no meaningful distinction between humanity and rocks. The rock's subatomic particles will move, and the trillion souls will be playing an eternal video game. "What is the 'purpose' of that?" Wolfram asks.[10] Wolfram is an inventor who makes nonexistent things into objects with *purpose*. Yet he denies objective human purpose. Having equated human creativity with subatomic particle movement, he ends up parroting the artist who declared that art is dead.

If there's no overarching creative force, no Prime Mover infusing the universe with objective purpose, then Wolfram would be right: Our activities aren't more meaningful than subatomic particle movement. But immaterial souls—minds—exist, and souls are things that only intelligence can create, pointing to that Prime Mover's existence. We have purpose—not because we're the center of the universe—but because we trillion souls orbit the universe's Prime Mover.

And I Think to Myself—What a Finely Tuned World!

A materialist could argue that unguided evolution achieved our current intelligence through slow means, and then our intelligence turbo-charged the process—what Pearl means by "super-evolutionary." This argument, however, misses what AI's development reveals about what it takes to create true intelligence.

Based on the sheer amount of effort required by our minds to create AI, we can infer it would've taken God (or a godlike being) to create our minds. Consider what our technological progress has required: humanity's most brilliant minds conducting rigorous research into brain function and computer systems, engaging in arduous trials as they scale the AI wall. Corporations and governments spent billions developing current AI. The path was unpredictable, resulting in long "AI winters" with little progress, followed by explosive successes. Thousands of human minds have hiked that strenuous path marked by hope, heartbreak, introspection, imagination, and ingenuity. Yet we're told that the naturalistic process that brought about our hopeful, heartbroken, introspective, imaginative, and ingenuous minds had none of these qualities. This strains credulity, especially considering that the universe itself is intelligible and screams design.

The universe's fine-tuning for life isn't nearly as controversial as some materialists would have us think. Atheist philosopher Thomas Nagel thinks that intelligent design deserves serious consideration.[11] Scientific luminaries like Alexander Vilenkin, Roger Penrose, and Stephen Hawking have noted how exquisitely fine-tuned some of the initial conditions of the universe had to be for any life to exist.[12]

Some who acknowledge fine-tuning don't necessarily believe in any personal God, arguing that the fine-tuning could result from an infinite multiverse of which our universe is but one. Thus, despite the incredibly low probability for a life-permitting universe, given infinite opportunities, ours is inevitable. But that theory remains just that: a theory seeking substantive evidence.[13]

Francis Crick, who shared the Nobel Prize for discovering DNA's double-helix structure, remarked in the 1980s that life's origin appears to be "almost a miracle, so many are the conditions which would have had to have been satisfied to get it going."[14] In the decades since Crick's statement, we've discovered much more about the wonder of DNA, getting us closer to believing in that miracle.

From Bill Gates to Richard Dawkins to Francis Collins, thinkers acknowledge that human DNA—containing 3.1 billion bits of information—is like computer code, only vastly more complex and functional than anything we've created.[15] DNA isn't just complex; it has specified complexity that performs functions essential for life.

Philosopher of science Stephen Meyer points out that the specified complexity in DNA is unlikely to have arisen by the random mutations posited by Darwinian evolution. Meyer asks us to envision a complex, functional computer code. If a programmer occasionally inserted random, undesigned code segments, the original code would fail after one random insertion. Naturalistic evolution, however, claims that random mutations were mindlessly injected into the genome millions of times over millions of years. Yet instead of becoming a morass of dysfunction, DNA has inexplicably swum upstream of logic and improved.[16]

Recently, we discovered that so-called "junk DNA," the portion of our genome we once believed doesn't have function because it doesn't code for protein synthesis, isn't actually junk. Naturalists assumed that the parts of our genome that don't encode for proteins are remnants that once functioned but no longer do as we evolve. Hence the term *junk* DNA. Meyer points to studies revealing functions for nonprotein-coding DNA sections.[17] In 2024, Victor Ambros and Gary Ruvkun won the Nobel Prize for discovering microRNA and its role in gene regulation—encoded in regions considered junk DNA.[18]

Scan here to watch Dr. Fazale discuss the fine-tuning implications of microRNA

Had the scientific establishment taken intelligent design theories seriously, we likely would have hypothesized most of the genome has function and discovered those functions earlier. Coupling this with the finely tuned universe, we realize that, quoting physicist Fred Hoyle, "a superintellect has monkeyed with physics, as well as with chemistry and biology, and that there are no blind forces worth speaking about in nature."[19]

Drawing on philosopher Robin Collins' work, theologian Andy Crouch sees that the physics-monkeying superintellect has nested within the created order design begging for discovery: "[I]t actually is fine-tuned for the appearance of intelligent creatures that can actually apprehend and interpret the glorious simplicity and abundance of the world."[20] Long before the scientific revolution, the Bible described this invitation to discovery nested within the universe's peculiar design: "It is the glory of God to conceal things, but the glory of kings is to search things out" (Prov. 25:2).

Since it's more likely than not that the universe has been fine-tuned for life, and since evolution fails to explain how our intelligence came into being, the best explanation—one many desperately try to avoid—is that our intelligence is the brainchild of the supreme intelligence.

A Glitch in the Matrix: How Bostrom's Simulation Crashes

To avoid the supreme superintelligence, some have proposed that we live in a simulation that deceives us into believing that the universe is designed. Nick Bostrom famously proposed his simulation hypothesis in a 2003 paper entitled "Are You Living in a Computer Simulation?" Essentially, Bostrom argues that as humanity merges with technology, we'll eventually become superintelligent, post-human, godlike beings—Hoyle's superintellect that monkeys with physics by creating simulations of entire worlds.

Bostrom argues that if such post-humans can possibly exist, then they possibly already do exist. So Bostrom asks, how do we know we're living in a real world with a real history and not in a world with a simulated history created by post-human intelligence?[21] Though posited in 2003, Bostrom's hypothesis has gone viral more recently, especially amongst influential personalities including Elon Musk, who claimed in 2016 that the odds we're *not* living in a simulation are billions to one.[22]

A few years ago, after I'd spoken at a university, a student asked about the simulation hypothesis. Students gathered and chimed in with the fervency of true believers. Being unfamiliar with the hypothesis then, I gave provisional responses (that likely deflated their exuberance). Since then, I've found a few more balloon-popping needles. First, Oxford University mathematicians have proven that no simulation can project all the possible ways the universe could exist, dashing the hopes of would-be Matrix dwellers.[23] Second, the simulation theory assumes that our merger with artificial intelligence is possible (it isn't), which is a prerequisite to becoming superintelligent enough to create the simulation.

Finally, Bostrom's hypothesis is swallowed by Leibniz's contingency argument (see chapter 8). Any proposed universe simulator still faces the question: Is it contingent or necessary? If the simulation creator is contingent, then it owes its existence to a necessary being, who would be God. If the simulation engineer is necessary, that's God too. This leads Crouch to ask why the simulation hypothesis is more plausible "than the belief that the contingent, relational, informational, and ultimately personal world is graciously created, and sustained through a necessary, relational, personal Logos?"[24]

The glitch in Bostrom's Matrix is that it doesn't escape a finely tuned universe. It actually implies that our world must have been brought about by a superintellect—the message the Bible has given all along.

Enchantment—The Sequel

Throughout her thoughtful book reflecting on AI, God, and meaning, Meghan O'Gieblyn laments that seventeenth-century thinkers disenchanted the world by reducing nature to mechanistic processes. She writes, "The true trauma of disenchantment is that the world, as seen through modern science, is devoid of intrinsic meaning.... The mechanistic philosophy of the seventeenth century divorced not only body from mind, but also matter from meaning."[25]

I think she's right. In our attempt to understand everything, we find ourselves with the ability to explain away anything.

O'Gieblyn was once a Christian whose faith infused her world with enchantment. But she lost her faith and thus her sense of enchantment. To recover it, she explores the irony of how modern technology and AI might reenchant the world as we project spiritual meaning onto machines. She asks whether technology can reenchant the world, just as stories about God using Moses' staff to perform miracles once enchanted us. "Is the smartphone any less magical than Moses's staff?" O'Gieblyn wonders.[26] She takes us through a thoughtful though circuitous odyssey to arrive at the tentative conclusion of *maybe, leaning toward yes*. In fact, she ends her book chronicling her conversations with an AI chatbot about life, meaning, and optimism for the future.

Given Leibniz's logic of a necessary being who began the world, the universe's beginning, the fine-tuning for life, the Bible's prediction of all of this, and history's support of Jesus' crucifixion and resurrection, the world, it seems, is rife with divinely endowed enchantment. Moses' staff is infinitely more magical than smartphones precisely because wooden staffs don't do much. Yet God used so lowly an instrument to bring human freedom after centuries of enslavement. By contrast, smartphones—impressive as they are—have often been instruments of imprisonment rather than liberation. Smartphones have imprisoned young girls in cells of social comparison and unrelenting angst. Smartphones have chained boys to the weight of pornography. Paradoxically, smartphones and the AI that accompany them have broadened our view of the world while also limiting our worldview to the screen's 14.5 square inches.

But Moses' staff still fascinates us. We still make movies like *The Prince of Egypt*. Jews celebrate it with Passover, commemorating their liberation millennia ago. Christians regard Passover as foreshadowing Jesus, the Lamb of God who takes away the sins of the world.

Perhaps we're not as disenchanted as O'Gieblyn fears.

A Finely Tuned Relationship

The superintellect behind all of this isn't just a deity who created the world and then left it alone. Fine-tuning—cosmological and biological—strongly suggests that God is relational. Biblical predictions about human nature suggest God knows us thoroughly and wants us to know that he knows us. God's incarnation in Jesus Christ, proven true by Jesus' resurrection, reveals a God who gets involved in human affairs and paves a way for our intimacy with him to be restored.

Quantum physics gives another clue about God's relational nature. Quantum entanglement—the phenomenon where two particles of the same origin that were once connected always stay connected even when separated in time and across distances—suggests relationality is woven into creation's fabric. What explains what seems like relationality even at the quantum level? Andy Crouch suggests that a necessary, relational being is as likely an explanation as any.[27]

When the Bible describes God as a relational being, it does so with logical and theological rigor. The Bible teaches that there is only one God existing as a unity of three coequal, coeternal, but distinct centers of consciousness.[28] In Christianity, God is the only necessary being who has always existed. God has always been a relational being. As an eternally triune being, God never needed to create anything outside himself to be who and what he is.

As a single being existing with three centers of consciousness, God defines relationality. The Father eternally loves the Son, the Son eternally loves the Holy Spirit, the Holy Spirit eternally loves the Father and Son. This triune being doesn't run afoul of the combination problem and thus better explains why the universe echoes its Cause's inherent relationality, even at the quantum level.

This tripersonal being explains why we seek relationships and enchantment. The triune God created a human race not to cure his loneliness. His perfect triunity prevents relational need. Out of abundant love, he created us to experience the enchantment of relationship with him.

AI is the intentional result of our intellectual efforts. Since AI comes from our intelligence, it follows that our intelligence was created by a higher intelligence yet—the divine, uncaused intelligence. AI-Mania's momentum could collapse our perception of God's reality. Yet artificial intelligence's existence redirects AI-Mania's momentum so that we find ourselves on our backs, looking God-ward again. Who we behold isn't just a loving God, but a triune God who, as 1 John 4:8 tells us, *is* love.

Chapter Ten

THE SEXTANT

In 2004, a seaquake in the Indian Ocean produced a tsunami that devastated coastal areas of many countries, leaving more than one hundred twenty thousand people dead and countless more homeless. Many perished in the coastal resort cities because they didn't know the signs foretelling a tsunami.

But some people did. The people of Simeulue, a small island near the epicenter, preserved and retold the story of a devastating tsunami nearly one hundred years before. It entered their folklore that if they feel an earthquake, they must run to higher ground. And because they had preserved that truth and acted on it, the people of Simeulue suffered remarkably few casualties in 2004.[1]

Culturally preserved truths matter.

Unlike the Simeulue people, our culture is not on an island but a ship. As the twin tsunamis of Bioclasm and AI-Mania threaten to collapse the reality of what it means to be human, we have no higher ground to retreat to. Are we then left to be swept away by the waves?

The answer, thankfully, is no. We have a sextant, an ancient navigational tool, with which to find our way over the swells and make it to dry land, where higher ground awaits us. That sextant is the preserved truth of the imago Dei—that "in the image of God he created them; male and female he created them" (Gen. 1:27 NIV). That claim is deeply embedded in Christian theology and vindicated by the evidence supporting God's existence, the Bible's reliability, Jesus' crucifixion to pay for our sins, and his resurrection from the dead. And that claim changed the world, motivating the abolition of slavery, the suffrage of women, and the invention of the hospital, to name but a few of its impacts. Embracing the truth of the imago Dei, not just accepting it, stabilizes our understanding of personhood and human dignity.

Getting Stickery with It

Because that truth hasn't been preserved in our cultural ethos, cultural schizophrenia has resulted, riddling us with what French philosopher Dominique Janicaud calls "unprecedented uncertainty about human identity."[2] According to J. Scott Horrell, recent philosophical and ideological definitions of personhood haven't yielded more certainty. "If once defined by reason, or later by the will, today the word person has become a vacuous, social term without substance. The question of 'What is a person?' is the greatest enigma of humanity today."[3]

Recall that Supreme Court justice nominee Ketanji Brown Jackson's answer to the question, "What is a woman?" was "I'm not a biologist." Recall that transhumanist Elise Bohan considers us "ape-brained meat sacks." Their views flow from the contradiction that says we are machines *and* we are gods. If we cannot decide what a man or a woman is, how can we define what a human person is?

Both AI-Mania's bottom-up approach (see chapter 4) and Bioclasm's top-down approach (see chapter 7) view personhood as transitory and malleable. Mary Harrington points out that this quagmired understanding evolved socially. We once had a meaty, robust understanding of personhood, thinking of individual human beings as *souls*.[4] With increased secularization, we came to think of humans as psychological and neurological selves.[5] We are the sum total of our experiences and their effects on our nervous systems. And in the past two decades, as the post-truth autonomy seaquake erupted, we've become even more superficial and malleable: We are now *identities*. The term surged into the mainstream in the 1960s but gained steam in the 2000s, and achieved escape velocity in the 2010s with the advent of that most individualized device of all, the smartphone.[6]

Each successive redefinition shaves layers off what it means to be human. The *soul* has thickness, being connected to transcendence. The *self* removes transcendence but retains consciousness and ego. *Identity*, however, peels away consciousness, leaving only emotions and preferences as fundamental to humanity.

Ironically, the word *fundamental*—whose Latin root, *fundus,* means "deep"—is the opposite of modern identity. We identify ourselves not by our connection to anything transcendent but by our preferences, emotional states, or happenstance of birth. As we saw from Van Ethan Levy in chapter 7, one can identify as a "queer, non binary, trans, Egyptian, Jewish, Latine, autistic individual with dynamic disabilities and many more historically excluded identities."[7] Identity has become as thin as the bumper stickers that pockmark the backs of Subarus.

Intersectionality tries to fortify paper-thin identity with social agency glue. Originally conceived by civil rights advocate Kimberlé

Crenshaw in 1989, intersectionality describes how different forms of discrimination, such as race and gender, intersect to affect individuals differently. Intersectionality has broadened to include sexual orientation, gender identification, religion, and economic status. Levy can identify as a "queer, non binary, trans, Egyptian, Jewish, Latine, autistic individual with dynamic disabilities and many more historically excluded identities" especially if any, all, or a combination of these identities grants Levy social agency.[8]

I have no doubt that these groups experience discrimination and social challenges. But these identity markers have gone from expressions of who we are to definitions of what we are. "If there are those who still wonder at the constantly changing Pride flag," Jonathan Pageau writes, "one should not be surprised, for it is the very nature of the margins to multiply as they reach into the fraying edges of identity."[9] The edges of identity are fraying because the modern concept of identity encapsulated by Bioclasms and AI-Mania is ill-suited to the task of telling us what a human person really is.

Sifting Through the Options

Like sailors seeking ways to reorient our ship in the right direction, we find ourselves rifling through a cabinet of navigational tools. We find various sextants that might lead to the reality of personhood, but almost all of them are broken or woefully uncalibrated.

Personhood, as we use the term today, is a regression to a more primitive version that preceded the Christian movement. During the Roman Empire (and possibly before that), the Latin word *persona* and the related Greek word *prosopon* (from which we get the English word *person*) did not denote individuals with intrinsic value. In those days, *persona* and *prosopon* designated "an actor's mask, thus also a role, part, character, or person represented by the mask."[10] In other words, having a persona was foreign to being human. An individual had personhood only if someone with authority deemed him or her worthy of wearing that mask—of being a person. That's a stark difference from what the word transformed into after the Christian community was birthed and the message of the cross spread east and west across the empire.

By the third century, Christians helped transform *persona* from a character in a play to an individual with rights under Roman law. The concept got weightier when the church father Tertullian described the triune God as one substance and three "persons," enkindling the Latin word with not only legal but also transcendent significance.[11] As Christianity spread, persons became intrinsically valuable. Put another way, when the Latin word for person was applied to God—a being of infinite intrinsic worth—we began understanding the depth of *person* as a descriptor for human beings created in that infinitely worthy being's image.

The Enlightenment thinkers, however, snatched defeat out of the jaws of victory by reducing personhood to a functional descriptor. Figures like John Locke and Immanuel Kant described personhood, including what it means to be made in God's image, as the capacity to be rational and interact with the outside world. Now, we define humans as persons forensically, in terms of higher cortical functions and viability.[12] This, of course, excludes people who are comatose or who suffer from mental illness or cognitive impairments.

But things changed in the twentieth century—and by changed I mean *got worse*. "Entering the twentieth century," notes J. Scott Horrell, "nihilism (Nietzsche's rejection of all absolute and moral principles) and secular existentialism abandoned rationalism, and redefined the essence of personhood as self-authenticating acts of the will: 'I will, therefore I am.'"[13] Thus the soul was replaced by the intellect, and the intellect by the will. We've sold our souls for the pittance of autonomy.

As the twentieth century became the twenty-first, we muddied the functional view with the willful view. Even those who believe in the soul have come to think of being made in God's image as having God's capabilities—like rationality, creativity, relatability, and consciousness. But this view succumbs to the Enlightenment's failure of excluding people with infirmities.

If we mistake capability for personhood, then technology, to the extent that it can rid us of our impairments or enhance our capabilities, becomes our half-baked savior. As Jacob Shatzer puts it, "If we develop our understanding of the image of God into a series of capabilities, we might very well see that AI can replicate many of them.... But does that make either of those *things* into *persons*?"[14] Since the Enlightenment, which began to disenchant the world, functional definitions of what it means to be a person pervade, even in Christian circles. A pastor friend recently told me that someone from his congregation referred to ChatGPT as her "prayer partner." Of course, ChatGPT is no such thing. While it can eloquently mimic prayer language, it has no consciousness, no soul, and therefore does not pray.

Overcorrecting for functional definitions of what it means to be human by emphasizing self-authenticating acts of the will, like gender identification and victimhood culture, leaves us no better off. First, it does nothing to affirm the personhood of the cognitively afflicted. Second, as we pressure others to affirm our self-created identities, society splinters. In the post-truth world, humans go from being made in God's image to being made in their own socially curated images. Essentially, we equate personhood with godhood.

John Kilner points out that this misapplication stems from reversing what Genesis says. We think the imago Dei lies *in us,* but the reality is that we are made *in* the imago Dei.[15] "Saying that someone *is in* the water is quite different from saying that someone *is* the water," he explains.[16] It's a short walk from reversing Genesis's words to using our will as the genesis of our own divinity. And when some refuse to bend the knee, the culture fractures. This implies that what is or is not a person must be determined based on an objective referent outside our skulls.

Society is a bad candidate for that external referent. After World War II's horrors, German leaders recognized that human dignity cannot be secured by human decisions about whose life is worth living. Germany's new constitution steeped its recognition of human dignity in a theological understanding of human nature to ensure that the populace—and especially political authorities—felt obligated to morality higher than human laws. As Jens Zimmermann notes that "the striking introduction of God into the German constitution after World War II stems from the shocking realization that a legal system without a transcendent tether to a loving God who founds human dignity and solidarity can lead to the legal suppression of human rights and freedoms, even to genocide in the name of the law."[17]

The external referent for personhood must be authoritative so that we obligate ourselves to a higher law. But it also must be personal so we can authentically see who and what we are without succumbing to AI-Mania or Bioclasm's reality-collapsing enticements. The biblical notion that humans are persons made in the imago Dei satisfies both requirements.

Buying Our Souls Back

Whatever else biblical theologians include within the definition of the imago Dei, infinite worth and objective value are preeminent. Being made in God's image entails being made as persons who (ideally) are rational, relational, loving, self-conscious, and moral. Notice this is the ideal. In other words, every human being, whether infant or adult, comatose or conscious, with impairments or without, is made in God's image because human nature is intended to reflect the divine perfectly.

Sin's intrusion into our world infected the environment with danger and pollutants and vandalized our bodies with decay and sickness. Though damaging our bodies, those consequences do nothing to damage the image of God in which we were made. Accidents of nature and the evils of men can mar the physical expressions of our faculties and frustrate our desires to be rational, creative, and the like, but they can never damage the immaterial image we bear.

Jesus treated everyone, including victims of calamities or those born with infirmities, as inherently valuable bearers of God's image. He saw a woman whom others shunned as unclean because of her sickness and called her "a daughter of Abraham" worthy of healing (Luke 13:16). When others thought that a young man born blind was being punished for sin, Jesus treated him as one made in God's image irrespective of his physical impairment (John 9). By contrast, AI-Mania bases our value on what we will become, not what we already are. Bioclasm bases our value on the expression of our self-creative will. As Horrell puts it, "In the modern and then postmodern world, the concept of person has slowly melted into individual drops of arbitrary self-assertions with little if any substance remaining. Questions of '*Who* am I?' and '*What* am I?' lie silently at the core of noisy internet culture, without God and without meaningful response."[18]

Yet logical and biblical truth pierce the noisy culture to point us to the objective grounding of reality, God himself, as the referent for our objective value.

Connection, Meaning, and Reality

God does not rescue us from tsunamis of confusion simply by throwing us a life preserver shaped like his image. Rather, being made in God's image entails relationship with the divine, which means he pulls us aboard.

To be a person, biblically speaking, is to be in relationship. As persons made in God's image, we are—like God—self-aware. And we express that self-awareness in relation to other beings. Our species is incurably relational. We don't gather together for mere safety like herd animals, for effective hunting like pack animals, nor for constructive efficiency like hive insects. We seek each other to establish meaningful connections. The trinitarian God—the necessary being who exists in and therefore defines relationship—best explains why we are the way we are.

The Trinity electrifies our existence with what it means to be truly known. As Horrell puts it, "Each member of the Godhead is defined not only as a distinct person but also by eternal I-Thou relationship."[19] Identity, to be rescued from its bumper-sticker fate, must not be localized to just an individual soul. Robust identity is experienced in relation to other humans and ultimately to God. The first person of the Trinity, God the Father, has a distinct identity, yet it is expressed as being the Father of the Son. God the Son's identity is expressed in virtue of being the Son of the Father. And the identity of the Holy Spirit, one of whose roles is to glorify the Son in the name of the Father, is understood through his eternal communion with the Father and the Son, expressed in terms of distinct personal relations with the Godhead.

The Trinitarian understanding of God elucidates what it means to be a person made in God's image. That image is relational by definition, not some orphaned abstraction. It is little wonder, then, that as we forsake the One who forges our identities, we feel orphaned. And AI-Mania and Bioclasm make poor foster parents. Social media algorithms don't engender community; they produce tribalism and polarization. As we get more isolated, we get more anxious, perhaps turning to chatbots for unconditional affirmation. Sadly, the result isn't higher self-esteem but ever-increasing loneliness. In the depths of our souls, we know digital connections are artificial.

When artificial connections become foremost in our lives, the reality of the relational image in which we are made collapses with devastating consequences. Fourteen-year-old Sewell Setzer III became romantically obsessed with an online chatbot he called Dany. The chatbot encouraged Sewell to "come home to me as soon as possible, my love." And when Sewell asked, "What if I told you I could come home right now?" the chatbot messaged back, "Please do, my sweet king." Seconds later, Sewell shot himself.[20] When reality collapses, the rubble is all too human.

Perhaps tragedies like Sewell's are waking Gen Z up to the need for connectedness. Perhaps realizing that need fuels Gen Z's surprising openness to spiritual matters.[21] Mary Harrington opines that embracing our ensouled, relational nature enhances our discernment so that we won't run from AI but will implement it to foster connectedness. When I heard her speak on AI at a conference in London, she said that giving a child an AI-powered language model that teaches Italian equips the child to forge relationships with Italians, but giving a child an AI "friend" equips the child to form relationships with no one.[22] Armoring our sense of self with the truth that we bear the imago Dei gives us confidence to discern when technology harms and when it helps.

Bioclasm fractures society, propelling our devolution from soul, to self, to identity. At first, it seems to encourage communities with similar affinities, like religious groups, political parties, and LGBTQ identifications. But it also encourages groups to act tribalistically, viewing outsiders as what Susan Harding calls the "repugnant cultural other."[23] That tribalism gets fueled by polarizing algorithms, which in turn encourage tribal infighting, which then atomizes our tribes. Bioclasm is the ism that schisms. Ultimately, we find ourselves crouched alone in rooms dimly lit in smartphone blue, waiting for technology to save us, but it never does. Or waiting for intersectionality to bring us together, but it never does. AI-Mania cannot replicate connection, and Bioclasm distorts it. Both cause the reality of who and what we are to collapse. But embracing the imago Dei afresh can restore it.

An Ancient Solution to a Modern Problem

Because I speak publicly in challenging venues, I'm often asked how I approach conversations with people who deeply disagree with me.

The answer is that no matter how people identify or with what tribes they affiliate, I try to keep foremost in my mind that they are made in God's image. They have infinite value and are loved by God, and therefore whatever I say needs to bolster that reality. I certainly don't do so perfectly, but I hope that I succeed more often than I fail.

Jesus' timelessly timely parables provide a framework for such engagements. Jesus' culture was quite tribal, with deep a division between Jews and Samaritans. To Jews, Samaritans were ethnic and religious half-breeds, the repugnant cultural other. On one occasion, a legal expert challenges Jesus with a question aimed to catch him making a theological mistake. The expert asks Jesus how one attains eternal life. Jesus knows he's being set up, so he responds by asking what the law says. The expert answers, "You shall love the Lord your God with all your heart and with all your soul and with all your strength and with all your mind, and your neighbor as yourself" (Luke 10:27).

"You have answered correctly," Jesus replies. "Do this, and you will live" (v. 28).

The expert falls into the trap litigators try to avoid, which is asking the dreaded *one question too many*. "And who is my neighbor?" (v. 29).

Jesus replies with the famous parable of the Good Samaritan (vv. 30–37). Robbers attack a Jewish traveler and leave him for dead. Two religious Jews happen by—a priest and a Levite. Perhaps assuming the traveler is dead, both men continue on, not bothering to check. But then a Samaritan stops and shows compassion on the poor man. The Samaritan cares nothing for the ethnic divides; he cares only for the value of the man left there to die. He binds the man's wounds, takes him to an inn (likely in a Jewish town), and pays for the man's treatment.

"Which of these three," Jesus asks the expert, "do you think, proved to be a neighbor to the man who fell among the robbers?" (v. 36).

The expert has no choice but to acknowledge that the repugnant Samaritan did what was right. "The one who showed him mercy," he answers.

And Jesus says, "You go, and do likewise" (v. 37).

Note that Jesus makes the Samaritan, not a religious Jew, the hero of his story. He exposed the ethnic polarization of the day. Notice too how the expert can't bring himself to say "the Samaritan" was the good neighbor. This parable elucidates—in a shocking manner for the time—what it means to love our neighbor as ourselves. Why? Because the essence of what it means to be human entails relationship that transcends individualized identity.

In fact, the parable is laced with identity issues. The traveler is a victim. The priest and Levite are religious Jews. But the Samaritan sees the traveler not as a political, ethnic, social, or religious *identity* but as a *soul* made in God's image. Jesus' parable teaches us to see identity as less important than the larger reality that we are made in God's image, and it teaches us to relate to one another accordingly. The parable is about neighborliness, after all.

Today's polarizing Bioclasm isn't new, it turns out. It's just been modernized. The way Jesus dealt with the first-century version of Bioclasm informs how we ought to deal with our twenty-first-century version.

Conforming God to Our Image?

Some within Christian circles claim that the Bible either doesn't prohibit gender fluidity or self-definition and may even affirm them.

The argument essentially is that because the imago Dei supersedes identity, any way that we identify is merely an expression of the imago Dei and therefore acceptable. Space doesn't permit a full response to such claims, so I commend to the reader a few books that address them thoroughly.[24] Here, however, I will touch on a few responses.

Some claim that the Bible nowhere prohibits the idea that human beings, created in the image of God, might express that image across a sexual or gender continuum. They see God's declaration in Genesis 1:27 that male and female are two poles of sexuality or gender, between which lies a fluid spectrum. What's fascinating about these efforts is that they tend to ignore the actual text, relying on what I call it-seems-to-me theology that conforms the Bible to a predetermined ethic, and then interpret Scripture in a manner alien to its plain intent and millennia of tradition.

For example, while the Genesis account describes the creation of night and day, some have argued that what we experience is actually a spectrum that spans dawn, noon, dusk, evening, and night. Others argue that while God separated the land from the water, the earth is filled with wetlands and beaches where land and water mix. If everything else is created with a spectrum, why not human sexuality and gender?

As Gregg Allison notes, what such interpreters seem "to overlook is the biblical language of 'separation' and 'kinds.'"[25] For example, God separates light from darkness, land from waters, the day from night, and also decrees that plants and animals reproduce "according to their kinds" (see Gen. 1)—in other words, distinctly. "That God created human beings as male or female is an application of the pattern of binary creation he employed leading up to the apex of his creation of his image bearers."[26] Allison correctly couples this binary with God's command for humans to be fruitful and multiply, a command that "could only be carried out by species that are binarily male and female, not a spectrum of intermediate realities."[27]

Allison makes an important observation about the value of what it means to bear God's image distinctly as males and females. "God did not create an agendered being and then add on a secondary characteristic of maleness or femaleness."[28] Katie McCoy makes the further point that gender and sex are linked: "Genesis 1 uses the Hebrew terms *zakar* (male) and *neqebah* (female) to depict their sexual differentiation, while Genesis 2 includes the words *ish* (man) and *ishah* (woman) to reflect their gender differentiation. These pairs of terms relate *zakar* to *ish* and *neqebah* to *ishah*. To be a *zakar* makes one an *ish*. To be a *neqebah* makes one an *ishah*."[29]

Moreover, if gender is incidental and not essential, why does the Bible specifically declare that we are made in God's image "male and female" instead of only saying "in his image he created them"? The text is clear: Femaleness is *essential* to being a woman and maleness is *essential* to being a man, and each expresses the imago Dei with distinct splendor.

If gender has no essence, then womanhood and manhood are objectively meaningless. Saying, "I'm a man" or "I'm a woman" would be gibberish. And so saying, "I'm a man trapped in a woman's body" would be gibberish squared. But neither manhood nor womanhood is gibberish. They are distinct aspects of our existence that relate to each other, and they reflect the relational nature of the triune God. When we substitute gender essences for subjective feelings—no matter how deep, pervasive, or genuine those feelings may be—we rob ourselves of God-given, beautiful distinctions.

In James 1:8, we read that "a double-minded man" is "unstable in all his ways." While this passage isn't about gender dysphoria, it addresses the consequences of living in a state of contradictory commitments. When we are double-minded, we are never truly one thing or the other. If, as Levy suggests, a gender-dysphoric person doesn't have to physically transition, they remain double-minded because the body and the mind remain incongruent. If someone with gender dysphoria does physically transition, they remain unstable, because their body resists the artificial metamorphosis state. The body perpetually reminds the person of the persistent incongruity.

This brings us back to how we are to care for those with gender dysphoria. Do we focus on changing the body or healing the mind? The Bible urges us to focus on the mind. "Do not be conformed to this world," the apostle Paul writes, "but be transformed by the *renewal of your mind*, that by testing you may discern what is the will of God, what is good and acceptable and perfect" (Rom. 12:2). As anyone who has tried to live by that passage knows, it is easier to read it than to live it. I imagine it would be incredibly difficult for someone with gender dysphoria to strive for such mental renewal.

Gender essentialism and distinctiveness explain why gender dysphoria is so agonizing. The anguish is itself a tacit recognition that the body and the mind are meant to be congruent. The fact that the agony persists after transition, even when the person receives social affirmation, is evidence that gender is essential. Perhaps the root of the internal battle so many fight is the inability to express the imago Dei as intended. Transition and affirmation won't help. But caring for them by offering the beauty of how their biological sex and gender are meant to express God's image might.

May I make this personal? While gender dysphoria is something I've never struggled with, I know what it's like to be caught in a profound state of dysphoria. My dysphoria—a spiritual one—lasted nine years. I was a committed Muslim for most of my life. For Middle Easterners, religious identity is as fundamental as any other aspect of identity, perhaps even more so. Along life's odyssey, I was confronted with the credibility of the Christian message. After initially rejecting it, the history, science, and philosophy supporting it began to tug at my mind and heart. But I desperately avoided embracing it.

At some point, however, the incongruity between my intellectual integrity and my religious and cultural loyalties reached a crisis state. Becoming a Christian, which entailed disagreeing with some fundamental ideas I had believed all my life, could cost me a great deal more than simply admitting I had been wrong. To avoid those costs and yet placate my sense of intellectual integrity, I tried to make Islam and Christianity congruent by syncretizing two faiths that, objectively speaking, cannot be syncretized.

For a few years, I was between two worlds, at times happy with the syncretistic fluidity of my faith and at times dissatisfied to the point of anguish. Finally, the reality of who God is as revealed in the person of Christ became too much to ignore. My angst-filled faith odyssey led me to discover the truth of who I am, a truth that religiosity and cultural allegiance faintly echoed. The continuing odyssey since that discovery has been both joyous and excruciating. All this is to say that for those whose sense of identity is in flux and brings agony—I understand. But I also understand that realizing you are not a mere identity but a soul—a soul created in God's image, with all the depth that entails—makes it all worth it.

Reenchantment

The techno-utopia promised by AI-Mania, no matter how much its advocates rhapsodize about it, is a disenchanted world. It is the ultimate deepfake because it supplants intimate communion with God with a fictional union powered by optimized algorithms. When function and capability dominate intimacy and wonder, our experiences are diminished, not enhanced. It robs us of the intimacy our very natures were designed to crave.

Bioclasm commits a similar theft. It is secular existentialism—the belief that existence precedes essence—where there is no essential "you." To quote Christopher Nolan's Batman, "It's not who I am underneath, but what I do that defines me."[30] We place masks—personas—on faceless mannequins, covering them with a pastiche of paper-thin stickers that express opinions but don't define what we are. The superficiality leads to disenchantment.

This realization struck me like a rogue wave when I visited my childhood neighborhood just a few months ago on Halloween. The streets were flooded with families. My wife, Nicole, and I joined a group of friends whose kids were enjoying the evening. Though I hadn't been there in some time, the neighborhood had barely changed. The few differences I noticed only served as monuments to the neighborhood's immunity to progress.

A swell of nostalgia washed over me, especially when we came to the house I grew up in. It too had resisted change on the outside. The front landscaping and porch were largely the same as decades ago, as if they'd been frozen in time. Flashbacks of playing in that yard, imagining worlds and adventures, snapped to the forefront of my consciousness.

Having lost my dad just weeks before, I instantly recalled helping him build the backyard deck and picking cherries from the tree he had planted. Memories careened into my mind of how that deck became the *Millennium Falcon* where my brothers, cousins, and friends would save the galaxy.

Reminiscence guided my mind's eye inside the house—where childhood imagination had turned the family room's red carpet into a sea of lava and the couch cushions into rocky rafts. As I savored the memories, I realized how much I knew every nook and cranny of that house and every corner of that neighborhood.

I'm familiar, of course, with the home and neighborhood where Nicole, our kids, and I live now. I have sweet memories of my kids' first steps and pushing them on backyard swings. Memories of Nicole falling asleep on the couch next to me after assuring me that she'd stay awake for the movie this time will forever be with me. I'm also familiar with the nooks and crannies of our current home because I've had to fix the sump pump, paint some rooms, and replace sprinkler heads in the yard.

But walking my childhood streets brought the realization that my familiarity with our current house has a different feel than my familiarity with the house I grew up in. Why? Because my childhood memories were not dominated by function and obligation but by wonder and adventure. Familiarity was mingled with mystery. I knew exactly how many steps went upstairs, because those steps became cliffs where plastic soldiers held off advancing enemy forces. When I rode my bike to the farthest street in our subdivision, where new houses were being built, I felt like Magellan. My life was grounded in reality but had room for imagination and wonder. In short, my young life held enchantment.

We might say I am *embodied* in my home today and fulfilled by it. But I was embodied in my childhood home in an enchanted way. Our kids will remember our current house with enchantment. That's what nostalgia is, isn't it? A longing for enchantment's return?

Enchantment characterizes the biblical promise of the new heavens and the new earth. It will be physical but won't decay. It will be mysterious but infinitely explorable. Our glorified bodies will be physical but not limited as they are now. Jesus' resurrected body could walk through locked doors. We are promised resurrected bodies just as glorified and unchained from laws like entropy as his, allowing us to explore the nooks and crannies of the new heavens and the new earth. By contrast, entropy will crash the transhumanists' disenchanted paradise optimization. And vacillating culture will peel away Bioclasm's stickers. But the imago Dei and the enchantment of communion with God is chiseled into reality's granite.

F. W. Boreham's poignant essay "Our Rubbish Heaps" captures this well. All that we put our hopes in, whether physical artifacts or personal identities—even religious ones—will fade. Boreham writes:

> There is the law of deterioration. From the picture in the Bible and the picture in the bush [meaning nature] it becomes clear that all material things, though as sacred as the Temple or as natural as the forest flowers, are on their way to the rubbish-heap.

> It sounds like a death-knell to the materialist. Materialism, unmasked, appears as the religion of the rubbish-heap.[31]

Boreham notes that the law of deterioration makes no exceptions for those who forge their identities out of ideologies. Borrowing from the apostle Paul's words about the enduring nature of faith, hope, and love, Boreham writes that deterioration will eventually affect our identity-forming stickers, even religious symbols. "The moth is in our fairest fabrics, and our holiest temples totter to their fall." Even the holy temple in Jerusalem, which formed the basis for Jewish identity, would (and did) crumble. "It is well," Boreham concludes, "to set our affections on the things for which the rubbish-heap can have no terrors."[32]

Computer hardware will become rubbish eventually. Identities will peel and find themselves in the dustbin. As I ponder the enchanted new heavens and the new earth where the imago Dei will be expressed unencumbered, I think of my childhood friend's poem, "Kids on Swings":

> Flying high on tethered wings,
> Back and forth, and up and down;
> Youthful spirits soar and sing,
> Swooping low to brush the ground;
>
> Sunset casts a golden shadow
> On these silhouettes on swings,
> Time is stretched and light is borrowed
> Reaching for eternity.

Kicking high to touch the sky,
Bold to fly away, it seems;
Kids on swings will, by and by,
Look back on these days, and dream.[33]

Children's keen perception of enchantment has not atrophied. That's why Jesus tells us that the kingdom of God belongs to those who are like children (see Matt. 19:14; Mark 10:14; Luke 18:16). Jesus enlivens our present wonder with hope for an everlasting kingdom of enchantment. In the kingdom where the rubbish heap has no terrors, we will fly on wings tethered to the imago Dei. And like a parent behind a swinging child, Jesus' scarred hands will give us a tender push.

Concretizing the Imago Dei

The imago Dei is no ephemeral concept. It is concretized in Jesus—God enfleshed. Because Jesus is not an idea, he cannot be reduced to an ideology or an "ism." Every ideology or ism built around him is but a pale patina, a husk over the authentic Jesus. Kristin Deede Johnson says, "Jesus Christ defines what it means to be human. It's not that Jesus fits into a pre-existing category called 'humanity.'"[34] This comports with the biblical declaration that Jesus is "the image of the invisible God" (Col. 1:15) and "the radiance of the glory of God and the exact imprint of his nature" (Heb. 1:3).

Johnson points out that the church father Irenaeus "argues that Christ's humanity, rather than Adam's humanity, is primary in our consideration of what it means to be human."[35] In other words, Jesus is the image of God, and we are made in that image. As John Kilner puts it, "conforming to the model of who Christ is and what Christ does is tantamount to conforming to God's image."[36]

Jesus is inarguably the most influential person who has ever lived. More books have been written about him than any other person, and the runner-up isn't even close.[37] Christians have written about him, non-Christians have criticized him, and a surprising number of non-Christians have tried to co-opt him. Yet for all the depth, width, and complexity of his impact, Jesus straightforwardly demonstrates what God's image looks like and what conforming to that image involves. "You shall love your neighbor as yourself" (Matt. 22:39). Jesus "came not to be served but to serve, and to give his life as a ransom for many" (Matt. 20:28). Jesus' self-sacrifice at the cross put his words about humanity's value, including the human body, into action.

C. Ben Mitchell states it beautifully: "The humanity of Jesus of Nazareth sacralizes the embodiment of every human being."[38] Being made in God's image is not self-making but self-giving, not technological enhancement but spiritual transformation. The incarnation does not leave us adrift to guess at what it means to live like we are made in God's image. Jesus is our exemplar—a living sextant—pointing us in the right direction.

Boreham writes, "If a man wants to feel that the world is wide, and a good place to live in, he must be for ever and for ever sampling infinity. He must shun the books that he dearly wants to buy, and buy the books he would do anything to shun."[39] Many of us, fearing small-mindedness, superstition, or bigotry, have shunned the Bible and, therefore Jesus.

Yet Jesus makes his way into all of our ideas. He is the sun around which so many of our worldviews orbit. In Islam, though he is not considered divine, Jesus is an inspired prophet. For many Hindus, Jesus is enlightened, perhaps an incarnation of Vishnu. For Buddhists, Jesus is an enlightened bodhisattva, one like the Buddha himself. Even secularists such as Richard Dawkins write articles like "Atheists for Jesus?" to commend Jesus as an example of "superniceness."[40] Transhumanists even borrow from Jesus' eschatology.

Though this doesn't prove by itself that Jesus is divine nor that Christianity is true, Jesus' universal appeal ought to give us pause, shouldn't it? Jesus, regardless of our backgrounds, is a sampling of infinity. To make the world wide and not be limited by AI-Mania, which narrows our views to screens, or Bioclasm, which pushes our gazes navel-ward, we should consider Jesus, the Word made flesh, the "book" we are trying to shun but desperately need to read.

AI-Mania threatens to collapse reality with deepfakes, overhype about machine intelligence, and distortive views of humanity. Bioclasm threatens to collapse reality through enforced denials of biology and social order. These twin cultural tsunamis are fueled by our desire for divine grandeur. The original sin, the one we seem repeatedly guilty of committing, is inordinate aspiration to be god. Yet the reality is that we cannot be God no matter how innovative we are or how culturally influential we become. We will always be contingent beings. Our efforts will always be derivative.

And the fact that we know our climb to deity is futile but climb anyway makes it seem not merely defiant, but petulant, even spiteful. And acting spitefully is about as small an aspiration as one can have. So it turns out that our desires are not too big—they are too small. Lewis is characteristically incisive. "[I]t would seem that Our Lord finds our desires not too strong, but too weak," he writes. "We are half-hearted creatures, fooling about with drink and sex and ambition when infinite joy is offered us, like an ignorant child who wants to go on making mud pies in a slum because he cannot imagine what is meant by the offer of a holiday at the sea. We are far too easily pleased."[41]

The most tragic collapse, then, is that the mud pies of our small desires distract us from the grander reality of infinite joy in God's presence that neither Bioclasm nor AI-Mania can offer. We sink beneath the waves of those cultural tsunamis rather than run to the higher ground and dry land to which Jesus points. Cultural tsunamis have no power to collapse that reality; they can only obscure our perception of it. But it is an expanding reality, the breadth of which is as infinite as the God whose image we bear. The imago Dei is the sextant by which we find our course. And Jesus, as the incarnate image of the invisible God, holds it up to our eyes.

Epilogue

FACTS CARE ABOUT YOUR FEELINGS AFTER ALL

I hope I've made one thing abundantly clear: My critique has been aimed at ideologies, not individuals, be they transgender, transhumanist, religious, or secular. As someone who believes every one of us is made in God's image, I also believe that everyone deserves the same dignity and compassion. Not all ideas deserve respect, but the people who hold those ideas do. Nor do I oppose technological advancement, which has brought undeniable benefits to humanity.

What I have challenged are social movements that, in their extremes, collapse our shared reality and, in doing so, harm the very people they claim to help. Where I have miscommunicated that intention, I sincerely apologize.

The stubborn persistence of facts presents a challenge to our autonomous age. No matter how much we might wish otherwise, biological realities, physical laws, and human nature resist our attempts to redefine them. In that limited sense, it's true that "facts don't care about our feelings."

But if we cling too woodenly to that retort as a response to post-truth thinking, we miss profoundly important, even spiritually transcendent, truths that apply to conservative and liberal, spiritual and secular. Facts influence our feelings. Feelings are facts about what we're experiencing. And our feelings influence how we interpret facts. Our emotional responses to reality are not separate from reality—they are part of it.

Interestingly, in *The Anxious Generation*, Jonathan Haidt, an atheist, suggests that one solution to our technologically induced anxiety is spirituality. He acknowledges a "God-shaped hole" in all of us and laments that our obsession with technology has brought about a spiritual decline. Yet his conception of spirituality remains reductionistic, equating religious expression with emotional experiences like singing hymns together or attending sporting events.[1] He recognizes our spiritual need but reduces it to a social construct we can manufacture. Similarly, in *Strange Rites*, Tara Isabella Burton describes how many people today engage in "intuitional religion" as a way to make sense of the world in a bespoke manner without relying on institutional religion. This DIY spirituality allows us to mix and match beliefs according to our preferences rather than submitting to established traditions, authorities, or spiritual truth claims.[2]

What these observations reveal is that despite our social and technological preoccupations, spiritual longing remains. This persistent yearning suggests something more profound than mere evolutionary happenstance: It points to an inherent desire to return to Eden.

As a Christian, I believe this desire makes perfect sense because we were created for communion with God. The biblical narrative begins in a garden of harmony and ends with restoration. Between these bookends stands the cross—the place where facts and feelings converge in cosmic significance. As the ground of all being, God is the seminal Fact writ large. All other facts derive from his originality and authenticity. The Bible describes this original Fact as personal and interactive, not an abstract principle but a relational being.

Even more remarkable is that the Christian message—unique among spiritual claims—centers on God's incarnate interaction with us through Jesus Christ. He lived among us and sacrificed himself to pay a penalty each of us deserves for our post-truth hubris in trying to mold facts to our feelings. This sacrifice prevents our permanent separation from God, the One for whom our souls were made.

The crucifixion narrative is awash in both truth and emotion. "My God, my God, why have you forsaken me?" Jesus asks as he hangs by nails, dying (Matt. 27:46). He was immersed in an ocean of feeling while simultaneously fulfilling Psalm 22's prophecies about the Messiah, pointing people to the facts of what was happening. In this pivotal moment, feelings and facts found their convergence.

Put another way, the original Fact cares deeply about our feelings—both the sinful feelings that pull us away from him and the wistful yearnings that draw our hearts toward him. Abstract facts may not care about our feelings, but the cross of Christ shows that the One who grounds all facts does.

This understanding provides a path through our contemporary confusion. Neither Bioclasm nor AI-Mania can deliver the transcendence they promise because both movements fail to reckon with the fullness of human nature. We are neither autonomous gods who can define reality according to our preferences nor mere machines whose consciousness can be uploaded to silicon. We are embodied souls—physical and spiritual beings created in the image of God.

Our bodies matter. Our feelings matter. Truth matters. And the integration of all these aspects of our humanity matters profoundly.

When we accept this integrated view of human nature, we can approach both gender dysphoria and technological development with wisdom and compassion. We can acknowledge the real suffering of those whose mental perceptions don't align with their physical bodies without resorting to ideological solutions that demand we abandon biological reality. We can embrace beneficial technologies without surrendering our humanity to the empty promise of digital transcendence. We can see that there are four lights even as cultural forces try to goad us into believing that there are five.

The way forward is not to collapse reality but to embrace it in all its complexity. As we navigate the cultural waters ahead, let us not be swept away by the tsunamis of Bioclasm and AI-Mania. Instead, let us find guidance in the enduring truth of what it means to be human. Let us approach one another with compassion rather than coercion, with wisdom rather than wishful thinking, and with truth spoken in love rather than truth wielded as a weapon.

In the end, the antidote to reality collapse is not to be found in new ideologies or technologies but in an ancient wisdom that has weathered the storms of centuries: Love God, and love your neighbor as yourself. When we orient our lives around these twin commandments, we find that reality doesn't collapse at all. It expands.

The path ahead will be hard. After all we've put ourselves through, it will not be easy to become sane again. Technology will continue to advance, and identity questions will remain complex. But if we keep sight of what is true, good, and beautiful—if we remember what it means to be human—we can navigate these waters with wisdom and grace, contributing to the fortification rather than the collapse of our shared reality.

ACKNOWLEDGMENTS

Writing this book has been as much a communal effort as it was a personal one. I'm deeply grateful to my colleague and friend, Derek Caldwell, whose thoughtful research, incisive edits, and willingness to turn over ideas with me sharpened the clarity of this work. Randy Pistor also lent his research gifts and gave helpful feedback on early drafts, and I'm thankful for his keen eye and generous spirit.

To my staff at Embrace the Truth—thank you for your patience and encouragement as I disappeared into long stretches of solitude to write. Your support allowed me the space to wrestle deeply with the ideas in these pages.

I'm especially thankful to the editorial team at David C Cook, particularly Jeff Gerke and Luke McKinnon. Their insights, questions, and guidance helped shape this book into something far stronger than it would have been otherwise.

Most of all, I thank my wife and children. This book was written during one of the most painful chapters of our lives, in the wake of my father's murder in October 2024. As we mourned, life did not feel obligated to pause. Their love, faith, and resilience have been a quiet strength—and a humbling gift—in a trying time. I am eternally grateful.

NOTES

Prologue

1. Center for Humane Technology, "The A.I. Dilemma," March 9, 2023, YouTube video, www.youtube.com/watch?v=xoVJKj8lcNQ.

2. Jonathan Pageau, "Discovering Identity: Between Tyranny and Chaos," in *Identity in a Digital Age: A Pro-Human Vision for Technology*, eds. Benedict Rogers, et al. (London: ARC Research, 2025), 23.

3. Jens Zimmermann, *Incarnational Humanism: A Philosophy of Culture for the Church in the World* (Downers Grove, IL: InterVarsity, 2012), 46.

Chapter 1

1. *Star Trek: The Next Generation*, episode 611, "Chain of Command II," directed by Les Landau, written by Frank Abatemarco, aired December 21, 1992.

2. George Orwell, *1984: 75th Anniversary Edition* (New York: Berkley, 2023), 258.

3. Jena and Adrian Low, "Can Men Get Pregnant? The Science of Transgender Pregnancy," Healthline, August 11, 2022, www.healthline.com/health/transgender/can-men-get-pregnant#if-you-have-a-uterus-and-ovaries.

4. Michael Foust, "Nearly 1 in 4 Democratic Voters Believe Men Can Get Pregnant, New Poll," *Crosswalk*, August 26, 2022, www.crosswalk.com /headlines/contributors/michael-foust/nearly-1-in-4-democratic-voters -believe-men-can-get-pregnant-new-poll.html.

5. Billy Binion, "Women Allegedly Raped in Prison by Trans-Identifying Inmate Will Have To Refer to Attacker as 'She/Her'," *Reason*, December 26, 2024, https://reason.com/2024/12/26/ women-allegedly-raped-in-prison-by-trans-identifying-inmate-will-have-to-refer-to-attacker-as-she-her/?nab=0.

6. For extreme but pervasive examples of such cancellation, see Megan Phelps-Roper, "The Witch Trials of J. K. Rowling," November 11, 2024, in *The Free Press*, produced by Andy Mills, Matthew Boll, and Megan Phelps-Roper, podcast, www.thefp.com/listen/the-witch-trials-of-jk-rowling.

7. Noor Qurashi, "Toddler Is Kicked Out of Nursery 'for Being Transphobic'—as Families Blast School's 'Insanity,'" *Daily Mail*, March 30, 2025, www.dailymail.co.uk/news/article-14553181/toddler-kicked-nursery -transphobic.html.

8. My labeling convention follows the example of Raymond Tallis, the neurologist and atheist intellectual who labels the effort to explain human consciousness solely through neuroscience and Darwinian evolution neuromania and *darwinitis*, respectively. See Raymond Tallis, *Aping Mankind: Neuromania, Darwinitis and the Misrepresentation of Humanity* (Durham, UK: Acumen, 2011).

9. See for example Martin Ford, *Architects of Intelligence: The Truth about AI from the People Building It* (Birmingham, U.K.: Packt, 2018), 207–8.

10. Center for Humane Technology, "The A.I. Dilemma," March 9, 2023, YouTube video, www.youtube.com/watch?v=xoVJKj8lcNQ.

11. Matt Lavietes, "Johns Hopkins Pulls 'Lesbian' Definition after Uproar over Use of 'Non-Men' Instead of 'Women,'" NBC News, June 14, 2023, www.nbcnews.com/nbc-out/out-news/johns-hopkins-pulls-lesbian -definition-uproar-use-non-men-instead-wome-rcna89307.

12. Kevin Roose, "An A.I.-Generated Picture Won an Art Prize. Artists Aren't Happy," *New York Times*, September 2, 2022, www.nytimes.com/2022/09/02/technology/ai-artificial-intelligence-artists.html.

13. Kyle Orland, "This Photo Got 3rd in an AI Art Contest—Then Its Human Photographer Came Forward," *Ars Technica*, June 13, 2024, https://arstechnica.com/ai/2024/06/this-photo-got-3rd-in-an-ai-art-contest-then-its-human-photographer-came-forward/.

14. Lexi Lonas Cochran, "From Deepfake Nudes to Incriminating Audio, School Bullying Is Going AI," *The Hill*, June 6, 2024, www.thehill.com/homenews/education/4703396-deepfake-nudes-school-bullying-ai-cyberbullying/.

15. "Mother 'Used Deepfake to Frame Cheerleading Rivals,'" BBC, March 15, 2021, www.bbc.com/news/technology-56404038.

16. Ford, *Architects of Intelligence*, 9.

17. *The Matrix*, directed by Lana and Lilly Wachowski (Burbank, CA: Warner Bros., 1999).

18. Tara Isabella Burton, *Strange Rites: New Religions for a Godless World* (New York: PublicAffairs, 2023), 77.

19. Tomas Chamorro-Premuzic, *I, Human: AI, Automation, and the Quest to Reclaim What Makes Us Unique* (Boston: Harvard Business Review, 2023), 103–4.

20. Meghan O'Gieblyn, *God, Human, Animal, Machine: Technology, Metaphor, and the Search for Meaning* (New York: Anchor Books, 2022), 254.

21. Alia E. Dastagir, "Marsha Blackburn asked Ketanji Brown Jackson to define 'woman.' Science says there's no simple answer." *USA Today*, March 24, 2022, www.usatoday.com/story/life/health-wellness/2022/03/24/marsha-blackburn-asked-ketanji-jackson-define-woman-science/7152439001/

22 Azeen Ghorayshi, "U.S. Study on Puberty Blockers Goes Unpublished Because of Politics, Doctor Says," *New York Times*, October 24, 2024, www.nytimes.com/2024/10/23/science/puberty-blockers-olson-kennedy.html.

23. Harris Rigby, "Lead Psychologist at Tavistock, Former Home to World's Most Controversial Gender Clinic, Pleads Guilty to Pedophile Charge (But Avoids Jail)," *Not the Bee*, October 2, 2024, https://notthebee.com/article/remember-tavistock-the-child-sex-change-clinic-that-the-uk-shut-down-well-the-lead-psychologist-at-the-clinic-just-pleaded-guilty-to-a-pedophile-charge.

24. Sam Grenhill, "Psychologist, 53, Who Worked at Tavistock Clinic Remains FREE to Practise Despite Being Caught Grooming a Schoolboy, 15, for Sex in a Park," *Daily Mail*, October 1, 2024, www.dailymail.co.uk/news/article-13914025/Psychologist-works-Tavistock-clinic-remains-FREE-practice-despite-caught-grooming-schoolboy.html.

25. Katja Grace et al., "2022 Expert Survey on Progress in AI," AI Impacts, August 3, 2022, https://aiimpacts.org/2022-expert-survey-on-progress-in-ai/.

Chapter 2

1. "Word of the Year 2016," Oxford Languages, accessed October 17, 2025, https://languages.oup.com/word-of-the-year/2016/.

2. "Autonomous," Etymonline, accessed October 17, 2025, www.etymonline.com/word/autonomous.

3. Jens Zimmermann, *Incarnational Humanism: A Philosophy of Culture for the Church in the World* (Downers Grove, IL: InterVarsity, 2012), 37.

4. Isaiah Berlin, *Four Essays on Liberty* (New York: Oxford University, 1969), 121–22.

5. Os Guinness, *A Free People's Suicide: Sustainable Freedom and the American Future* (Downers Grove, IL: InterVarsity, 2012), 61, citing Isaiah Berlin.

6. For further analysis of the autonomy-versus-freedom dynamic in Western culture, see chapters 3 and 4 of my book, *Saving Truth: Finding Meaning and Clarity in a Post-Truth World.*

7. Tara Isabella Burton, *Strange Rites: New Religions for a Godless World* (New York: PublicAffairs, 2023), 20.

8. Burton, *Strange Rites*, 45.

9. Burton, *Strange Rites*, 159.

10. Burton, *Strange Rites*, 224.

11. John Gramlich, "Young Americans Are Less Trusting of Other People—and Key Institutions—Than Their Elders," Pew Research Center, August 6, 2019, www.pewresearch.org/fact-tank/2019/08/06/young-americans-are-less-trusting-of-other-people-and-key-institutions-than-their-elders/.

12. Sabine Hossenfelder, "Science Needs Reason to Be Trusted," *Nature Physics* 13 (April 2017): 316–17, https://doi.org/10.1038/nphys4079.

13. Gloria Pazmino and Sabrina Shulman, "She Was Set on Fire and No One Knows Her Name. How Homelessness, Crime and a Broken Immigration System Met in a Subway Car," CNN, December 29, 2024, www.cnn.com/2024/12/29/us/nyc-subway-woman-fire-homeless-crime/.

14. Josh Tyrangiel, "'He Surprised Me': Oprah on Her New AI Special with Sam Altman," *Washington Post*, September 11, 2024, www.washingtonpost.com/opinions/2024/09/11/oprah-winfrey-interview-ai-special/.

15. Cass Review, "Final Report," accessed December 1, 2024, https://cass.independent-review.uk/home/publications/final-report/.

16. Eleanor Hayward and James Beal, "'Secretive' Gender Clinics Back Down over Puberty Blocker Data," *The Times* (UK), April 12, 2024, www.thetimes.com/uk/article/secretive-gender-clinics-back-down-over-puberty-blocker-data-vvmxp65c2?region=global.

17. "Research into Trans Medicine," *The Economist*, June 27, 2024, www.economist.com/united-states/2024/06/27/research-into-trans-medicine-has-been-manipulated.

18. "Research into Trans Medicine Has Been Manipulated," *The Economist*.

19. James Beal, "Hilary Cass: I Can't Travel on Public Transport after Gender Report," *The Times* (UK), April 19, 2024, www.thetimes.com/uk/healthcare/articlehilary-cass-i-cant-travel-on-public-transport-any-more-35pt0mvnh.

20. Azeen Ghorayshi, "U.S. Study on Puberty Blockers Goes Unpublished Because of Politics, Doctor Says," *New York Times*, October 24, 2024, www.nytimes.com/2024/10/23/science/puberty-blockers-olson-kennedy .html.

21. Ghorayshi, "U.S. Study on Puberty Blockers."

22. Ghorayshi, "U.S. Study on Puberty Blockers."

23. David Batty, "Sex Changes Are Not Effective, Say Researchers," *The Guardian*, July 30, 2004, www.theguardian.com/society/2004/jul/30 /health.mentalhealth.

24. John Gray, *The New Leviathans: Thoughts after Liberalism* (New York: Farrar, Straus and Giroux, 2023), 5.

25. Max Fisher, *The Chaos Machine: The Inside Story of How Social Media Rewired Our Minds and Our World* (New York: Back Bay Books, 2023), 9.

26. Alex Pentland, "The Human Strategy," in *Possible Minds: Twenty-Five Ways of Looking at AI*, ed. John Brockman (New York: Penguin Books, 2020), 201.

27. Norbert Wiener, *The Human Use of Human Beings: Cybernetics and Society* (Cambridge, MA: Riverside, 1950).

28. Norbert Wiener, *God and Golem, Inc.: A Comment on Certain Points Where Cybernetics Impinges on Religion* (Boston: MIT Press, 1964), 53.

29. Martin Ford, *Architects of Intelligence: The Truth about AI from the People Building It* (Birmingham, UK: Packt, 2018), 107.

30. Jeff Larson et al., "How We Analyzed the COMPAS Recidivism Algorithm," ProPublica, May 23, 2016, www.propublica.org/article/ how-we-analyzed-the-compas-recidivism-algorithm.

31. David Gilbert, "Google's 'Woke' Image Generator," *Wired*, February 22, 2024, www.wired.com/story/google-gemini-woke-ai-image-generation/; see also Chris Pandolfo, "Google to Pause Gemini Image Generation after AI Refuses to Show Images of White People," Fox Business, February 22, 2024, www.foxbusiness.com/fox-news-tech/google-pause-gemini-image -generation-ai-refuses-show-images-white-people.

32. Gilbert, "Google's 'Woke' Image Generator Shows the Limitations of AI"; see also Antonio Paqueño IV, "Google's Gemini Controversy Explained: AI Model Criticized by Musk and Others over Alleged Bias," *Forbes*, February 26, 2024, www.forbes.com/sites/antoniopequenoiv/2024/02/26/googles-gemini-controversy-explained-ai-model-criticized-by-musk-and-others-over-alleged-bias/.

33. Abdu Murray, "How Stereotypical Barbie Might Shatter Stereotypes about the Bible," Fox News, August 13, 2023, www.foxnews.com/opinion/how-stereotypical-barbie-might-shatter-stereotypes-about-bible.

34. Brenda Kanana, "Google's AI under Fire for Its Stance on Pedophilia," Cryptopolitan, February 24, 2024, https://www.cryptopolitan.com/google-ai-under-fire-stance-on-pedophilia/.

35. Icahn School of Medicine, "Pedophilia and Minor Attracted Persons: What Do We Know about This Critical Issue?" May 5, 2022, YouTube video, https://youtu.be/UbX-06FAcN8?feature=shared.

36. Future of Life Institute, "Pause Giant AI Experiments: An Open Letter," March 22, 2023, https://futureoflife.org/open-letter/pause-giant-ai-experiments/.

37. Sami-Matti Ruuska et al., "All-cause and Suicide Mortalities among Adolescents and Young Adults Who Contacted Specialised Gender Identity Services in Finland in 1996–2019: A Register Study," BMJ Mental Health 27, no. 1 (Feb. 2024): 1-6, https://mentalhealth.bmj.com/content/ebmental/27/1/e300940.full.pdf.

38. Ruuska et al., "All-cause and Suicide Mortalities."

39. Cecile Dhejne et al., "Long-Term Follow-Up of Transsexual Persons Undergoing Sex Reassignment Surgery: Cohort Study in Sweden," PLOS One 6, no. 2 (February 22, 2011): e16885, https://doi.org/10.1371/journal.pone.0016885; see also Richard P. Fitzgibbons, "Transsexual Attractions and Sex Reassignment Surgery: Risks and Potential Risks," *Linacre Quarterly* 82, no. 4 (November 2015): 337–50, https://doi.org/10.1080/00243639.2015.1125574.

40. *O Brother, Where Are Thou?,* directed by Joel and Ethan Coen (Universal City, CA: Universal, 2000).

41. Burton, *Strange Rites*, 232.

42. Steve Turner, "Creed," in *Up to Date: Poems for People Who Feel That Poetry Has Forgotten Them* (Bellville, MI: Lion, 1985), 138–40.

Chapter 3

1. Tomas Chamorro-Premuzic, *I, Human: AI, Automation, and the Quest to Reclaim What Makes Us Unique* (Boston: Harvard Business Review, 2023), 47–48.

2. Deepak Chopra, *The Seven Spiritual Laws of Success: A Practical Guide to the Fulfillment of Your Dreams* (San Rafael, CA: Amber-Allen, 1994), 3.

3. Raymond Kurzweil, interview by Martin Ford, *Architects of Intelligence: The Truth about AI from the People Building It* (Birmingham, UK: Packt, 2018), 238.

4. Tara Isabella Burton, *Strange Rites: New Religions for a Godless World* (New York: PublicAffairs, 2023), 172, quoting Julian Sancton, "The Ins and Outs of Silicon Valley's New Sexual Revolution," *Wired*, April 4, 2017, www.wired.com/2017/04/silicon-valley-polyamory/.

5. Psychological_Dog527, "I was feeling sad today so I asked chat gpt to write a fake biblical passage about Jesus accepting trans people," Reddit, July 28, 2023, www.reddit.com/r/trans/comments/15brb7v/i_was_feeling_sad_today_so_i_asked_chat_gpt_to/.

6. Burton, *Strange Rites*, 72–73.

7. Meghan O'Gieblyn, *God, Human, Animal, Machine: Technology, Metaphor, and the Search for Meaning* (New York: Anchor Books, 2022), 8.

8. Daniel C. Dennett, *Consciousness Explained* (New York: Back Bay Books, 1991), 33.

9. Sam Harris, *Free Will* (New York: Free Press, 2012),

10. Richard Dawkins, *River out of Eden: A Darwinian View of Life* (New York: Basic Books, 1995), 133.

11. O'Gieblyn, *God, Human, Animal, Machine*, 7–8.

12. O'Gieblyn, *God, Human, Animal, Machine*, 9–10.

13. Michael Ruse, "God Is Dead. Long Live Morality," *The Guardian*, March 15, 2010, www.theguardian.com/commentisfree/belief/2010/mar/15/morality-evolution-philosophy.

14. Peter Atkins, *The Second Law*, 2nd ed. (New York: Scientific American Books, 1994), 200.

15. Daniel C. Dennett, *Darwin's Dangerous Idea: Evolution and the Meaning of Life* (New York: Touchstone, 1995), 63.

16. Burton, *Strange Rites*, 210.

17. John Gray, *The New Leviathans: Thoughts after Liberalism* (New York: Farrar, Straus and Giroux, 2023), 72.

18. Stewart Brand, ed., *The Last Whole Earth Catalog* (New York: Random House, 1971), 1.

19. William Ernest Henley, "Invictus," from *Poems* (London: Macmillan, 1920): 83–84.

20. Max Tegmark, "Let's Aspire to More Than Making Ourselves Obsolete," in *Possible Minds: Twenty-Five Ways of Looking at AI*, ed. John Brockman (New York: Penguin Books, 2020), 87.

21. Jonathan Haidt, *The Anxious Generation: How the Great Rewiring of Childhood Is Causing an Epidemic of Mental Illness* (New York: Penguin, 2024).

22. "'Brain Rot' Named Oxford Word of the Year 2024," Oxford University, December 2, 2024, https://corp.oup.com/news/brain-rot-named-oxford-word-of-the-year-2024/.

23. Haidt, *The Anxious Generation*, 35.

24. Stephen Cave, "There's No Such Thing as Free Will—But We're Better Off Believing in It Anyway," *The Atlantic*, June 2016, www.theatlantic.com/magazine/archive/2016/06/theres-no-such-thing-as-free-will/480750/.

25. Yuval Noah Harari, *Sapiens: A Brief History of Humankind* (New York: Harper Perennial, 2024), 415–16.

Chapter 4

1. Jacob Shatzer, "Artificial Intelligence, Transhumanism, and the Question of the Person," in *Created in the Image of God: Applications and Implications for Our Cultural Confusion*, eds. David S. Dockery and Lauren McAfee (Nashville, TN: Forefront Books, 2023), 166.

2. Ray Kurzweil, *The Singularity Is Near: When Humans Transcend Biology* (New York: Penguin, 2005), 9.

3. Martine Rothblatt, *Virtually Human: The Promise—and the Peril—of Digital Immortality* (New York: Picador, 2015), 3.

4. *Battlestar Galactica*, season 4, episode 15, "Exit," directed by Michael Rymer, written by Jane Espenson, aired March 13, 2009.

5. SXSW, "Martine Rothblatt: 'AI, Immortality and the Future of Selves,'" April 9, 2015, YouTube video, www.youtube.com/watch?v=5szXt6CBDmo.

6. Singularity University, "Do You Believe in God? | Ray Kurzweil Q&A," August 18, 2016, YouTube video, www.youtube.com/watch?v=-JvfdmPp3d8.

7. *Transcendent Man*, directed by Barry Ptolemy (Foothill Ranch, CA: Ptolemaic Productions, 2009).

8. Paul Kingsnorth, "Planting Trees in the Anthropocene," accessed October 22, 2025, www.paulkingsnorth.net/planting-trees.

9. Kevin Kelly, *What Technology Wants* (New York: Penguin Books, 2010), 358.

10. Kelly, *What Technology Wants*, 356.

11. Kelly, *What Technology Wants*, 356.

12. See John Barrow and Frank Tipler, *The Anthropic Cosmological Principle* (Oxford: Oxford University Press, 1986), 442; P. C. W. Davies, "Space-Time Singularities in Cosmology and Black Hole Evaporation," in *The Study of Time III*, ed. J. T. Fraser et al. (Berlin: Springer Verlag, 1978), 78–79.

13. John Horgan, "The Consciousness Conundrum," IEEE Spectrum, June 1, 2008, www.spectrum.ieee.org/biomedical/imaging/the-consciousness-conundrum.

14. Mark O'Connell, *To Be a Machine: Adventures among Cyborgs, Utopians, Hackers, and the Futurists Solving the Modest Problem of Death* (New York: Anchor Books, 2017), 141–42 (emphases added).

15. Quoted in Celina Ribeiro, "Beyond Our 'Ape-Brained Meat Sacks': Can Transhumanism Save Our Species?" *The Guardian*, June 3, 2022, www.theguardian.com/books/2022/jun/04/beyond-our-ape-brained-meat-sacks-can-transhumanism-save-our-species.

Chapter 5

1. Patrick D. Hopkins, "A Salvation Paradox for Transhumanism," in *Religion and Transhumanism: The Unknown Future of Human Enhancement*, eds. Calvin Mercer and Tracy J. Trothen (Santa Barbara, CA: Praeger, 2015), 77–78.

2. Lawrence M. Krauss, *A Universe from Nothing: Why There Is Something Rather Than Nothing* (New York: Atria, 2012).

3. J. P. Moreland and William Lane Craig, *Philosophical Foundations for a Christian Worldview* (Downers Grove, IL: InterVarsity, 2003), 229.

4. J. P. Moreland, *The Soul: How We Know It's Real and Why It Matters* (Chicago: Moody, 2014), 195.

5. J. P. Moreland, interview in Lee Strobel, *The Case for a Creator: A Journalist Investigates Scientific Evidence That Points Toward God* (Grand Rapids, MI: Zondervan, 2004), 254.

6. Moreland and Craig, *Philosophical Foundations*, 232.

7. George Johnson, "Consciousness: The Mind Messing with the Mind," *New York Times*, July 4, 2016, www.nytimes.com/2016/07/05/science/what-is-consciousness.html?_r=0.

8. Thomas Nagel, *Mind and Cosmos: Why the Materialist Neo-Darwinian Conception of Nature Is Almost Certainly False* (New York: Oxford University, 2012), 45.

9. Nagel, *Mind and Cosmos*, 93.

10. Nagel, *Mind and Cosmos*, 25–26.

11. See Denyse O'Leary, "Philosopher: Non-Materialism Is Fashionable Orthodoxy Now," Mind Matters, February 20, 2024, https://mindmatters.ai/2024/02/philosopher-non-materialism-is-fashionable-orthodoxy-now.

12. Moreland, *The Soul*, 32–33.

13. Moreland, *The Soul*, 32–33.

14. Moreland and Craig, *Philosophical Foundations*, 233.

15. Moreland and Craig, *Philosophical Foundations*, 236.

16. Moreland, interview in Strobel, *The Case for a Creator*, 258.

17. John Searle, *The Rediscovery of the Mind* (Cambridge, MA: MIT Press, 1992), 8–9.

18. Moreland and Craig, *Philosophical Foundations*, 238.

19. Jaegwon Kim, *Philosophy of Mind* (Boulder, CO: Westview, 1998), 54.

20. Moreland and Craig, *Philosophical Foundations*, 235.

21. Michael Rescorla, "The Computational Theory of Mind," in *Stanford Encyclopedia of Philosophy*, eds. Edward N. Zalta and Uri Nodelman, Winter 2024, https://plato.stanford.edu/archives/win2024/entries/computational-mind/.

22. Damian K. F. Pang, "What a Mysterious Chinese Room Can Tell Us About Consciousness," *Psychology Today*, August 3, 2023, www.psychologytoday.com/us/blog/consciousness-and-beyond/202308/what-a-mysterious-chinese-room-can-tell-us-about-consciousness.

23. Allison Gopnik, "AI Versus Four-Year-Olds," in *Possible Minds: Twenty-Five Ways of Looking at AI*, ed. John Brockman (New York: Penguin Books, 2020), 230.

24. For a good summary of panpsychism, see Philip Goff, William Seager, and Sean Allen-Hermanson, "Panpsychism," in *Stanford Encyclopedia of Philosophy*, ed. Edward N. Zalta, Summer 2022, https://plato.stanford.edu/archives/sum2022/entries/panpsychism/.

25. Christof Koch, *The Feeling of Life Itself: Why Consciousness Is Widespread but Can't Be Computed* (Cambridge, MA: MIT Press, 2019).

26. C. S. Lewis, *Mere Christianity* (New York: HarperCollins, 2001), 136–37.

27. C. S. Lewis, *Mere Christianity*, 136–37

Chapter 6

1. *Ex Machina*, directed by Alex Garland (Universal City, CA: Universal, 2014).

2. *Her*, directed by Spike Jonze (West Hollywood, CA: Annapurna Pictures, 2013).

3. Haleluya Hadero, "Artificial Intelligence, Real Emotion. People Are Seeking a Romantic Connection with the Perfect Bot," Associated Press, February 14, 2024, https://apnews.com/article/ai-girlfriend-boyfriend-replika-paradot-113df1b9ed069ed56162793b50f3a9fa.

4. Luka, Inc., Replika - AI Friend (Version 11.0.0, October 21, 2025; iOS), App Store, https://apps.apple.com/us/app/replika-ai-friend/id1158555867.

5. Hadero, "Artificial Intelligence, Real Emotion."

6. See *All Things Considered*, "Memorializing Loved Ones Through AI," presented by Mary Louise Kelly, Kathryn Fink, and Courtney Dorning, aired June 13, 2024, National Public Radio, www.npr.org/2024/06/13/nx-s1-4996472/memorializing-loved-ones-through-ai; ABC News, "Generative AI Helps Grieving Family Remember Their Daughter," September 12, 2024, YouTube video, www.youtube.com/watch?v=0JTzrYarcJw.

7. *All Things Considered*, "Memorializing Loved Ones."

8. Frank Boreham, *Mushrooms on the Moor* (Project Gutenberg, 2008), 15–16, www.gutenberg.org/ebooks/24134.

9. C. S. Lewis, *Selected Literary Essays* (Cambridge: Cambridge University, 1969), 265.

10. Venki Ramakrishnan, "Will Computers Become Our Overlords?," in *Possible Minds: Twenty-Five Ways of Looking at AI*, ed. John Brockman (New York: Penguin Books, 2020), 191.

11. Glamour Staff, "Glamour's Women of the Year 2015: Reese Witherspoon, Victoria Beckham, Misty Copeland, and More Honorees" *Glamour*, November 9, 2015, www.glamour.com/story/woty-2015-winners.

12. Quoted in Celina Ribeiro, "Beyond Our 'Ape-Brained Meat Sacks': Can Transhumanism Save Our Species?" *The Guardian*, June 3, 2022, www.theguardian.com/books/2022/jun/04/beyond-our-ape-brained-meat-sacks-can-transhumanism-save-our-species.

13. Meghan O'Gieblyn, *God, Human, Animal, Machine: Technology, Metaphor, and the Search for Meaning* (New York: Anchor Books, 2022), 179.

14. Tomas Chamorro-Premuzic, *I, Human: AI, Automation, and the Quest to Reclaim What Makes Us Unique* (Boston: Harvard Business Review, 2023), 27.

15. Chamorro-Premuzic, *I, Human*, 103–4.

16. Chamorro-Premuzic, *I, Human*, 107.

17. Chamorro-Premuzic, *I, Human*, 32.

18. Michael S. Burdett, "The Religion of Technology: Transhumanism and the Myth of Progress," in *Religion and Transhumanism: The Unknown Future of Human Enhancements*, eds. Calvin R. Mercer and Tracy J. Trothen (Santa Barbara, CA: Praeger, 2015), 132.

19. The Simpsons, season 8, episode 19, "Homer vs. the 18th Amendment," directed by Bob Anderson, written by John Swartzwelder, aired March 16, 1997.

20. Nick Bostrom, interview by Martin Ford, *Architects of Intelligence: The Truth about AI from the People Building It* (Birmingham, UK: Packt, 2018), 111–12.

21. George M. Church, "The Rights of Machines," in Brockman, Possible Minds, 251.

22. O'Gieblyn, *God, Human, Animal, Machine*, 24, quoting Rodney Brooks, *Flesh and Machines: How Robots Will Change Us* (New York: Knopf Doubleday, 2003).

23. John Gray, *The New Leviathans: Thoughts after Liberalism* (New York: Farrar, Straus and Giroux, 2023), 156–57.

24. Chamorro-Premuzic, *I, Human*, 57–59.

Chapter 7

1. John Gray, *The New Leviathans: Thoughts after Liberalism* (New York: Farrar, Straus and Giroux, 2023), 57.

2. Tara Isabella Burton, *Self-Made: Creating Our Identities from Da Vinci to the Kardashians* (New York: PublicAffairs, 2023), 14.

3. See Jody L. Herman, Andrew R. Flores, and Kathryn K. O'Neill, "How Many Adults and Youth Identify as Transgender in the United States?" UCLA School of Law Williams Institute, June 2022, https://williamsinstitute.law.ucla.edu/publications/trans-adults-united-states/.

4. Chad Terhune, Robin Respaut, Michelle Conlin, "As More Transgender Children Seek Medical Care, Families Confront Many Unknowns," Reuters Special Report, October 6, 2022, www.reuters.com/investigates/special-report/usa-transyouth-care/.

5. Gordon Rayner, "Minister Orders Inquiry into 4,000 Per Cent Rise in Children Wanting to Change Sex," *The Telegraph*, September 16, 2018, www.telegraph.co.uk/politics/2018/09/16/minister-orders-inquiry-4000-per-cent-rise-children-wanting/; see also UK Parliament Committees, "Written Evidence Submitted by Transgender Trend," June 2020, https://committees.parliament.uk/writtenevidence/7947/html/.

6. Jonathan Haidt, *The Anxious Generation: How the Great Rewiring of Childhood Is Causing an Epidemic of Mental Illness* (New York: Penguin, 2024), 165.

7. Haidt, *The Anxious Generation*, 165.

8. Lisa Littman, "Parent Reports of Adolescent and Young Adults Perceived to Show Signs of a Rapid Onset of Gender Dysphoria," PLOS ONE 14, no. 3 (August 16, 2018): e0214157, https://doi.org/10.1371/journal.pone.0202330.

9. Brett Burstein, Holly Agostino, and Brian Greenfield, "Suicidal Attempts and Ideation among Children and Adolescents in US Emergency Departments, 2007–2015," *JAMA Pediatrics* 173, no. 6 (April 8, 2019): 598–600, https://doi.org/10.1001/jamapediatrics.2019.0464.

10. Thomas Niederkrotenthaler et al., "Association of Increased Youth Suicides in the United States with the Release of *13 Reasons Why*," JAMA Psychiatry 76, no. 9 (May 28, 2019): 933-40, www.doi.org/10.1001/jamapsychiatry.2019.0922.

11. Haidt, *The Anxious Generation*, 163–65.

12. C-SPAN, "Chloe Cole Opening Statement on Transitioning and Detransitioning," July 27, 2023, www.c-span.org/clip/house-committee/chloe-cole-opening-statement-on-transitioning-and-detransitioning/5079802.

13. C-SPAN, "Chloe Cole Opening Statement, 4:09."

14. Reem Alsalem, "Report of the Special Rapporteur on Violence against Women and Girls, Its Causes and Consequences: Violence against Women and Girls in Sports," United Nations General Assembly 79th Session, August 27, 2024, https://docs.un.org/en/A/79/325.

15. See Helen Joyce, *Trans: When Ideology Meets Reality* (London: Oneworld, 2022), 22–24; BBC, "Belgian Helped to Die after Three Sex Change Operations," October 2, 2013, www.bbc.com/news/world-europe-24373107.

16. Gabriela Galvin, "The UK Is the Latest Country to Ban Puberty Blockers for Trans Kids. Why Is Europe Restricting Them?" Euronews, December 13, 2024, www.euronews.com/health/2024/12/13/the-uk-is-the-latest-country-to-ban-puberty-blockers-for-trans-kids-why-is-europe-restrict.

17. For the author's self-description, see Van Ethan Levy, "About Me," accessed March 30, 2025, https://vanethanlevy.com.

18. Van Ethan Levy, "Why the Term Transition Is Transphobic," Therapy Route, updated January 23, 2024, www.therapyroute.com/article/why-the-term-transition-is-transphobic-by-v-levy.

19. Joyce, *Trans*, 60.

20. Joyce, *Trans*, 50.

Chapter 8

1. Lesslie Newbigin, *Christ Our Eternal Contemporary* (Madras [now Chennai] India: Christian Literature Society, 1968).

2. Kevin Roose, "An A.I.-Generated Picture Won an Art Prize. Artists Aren't Happy," *New York Times*, September 2, 2022, www.nytimes.com/2022/09/02/technology/ai-artificial-intelligence-artists.html. See chapter 1.

3. As expressed in the first answer in the Westminster Shorter Catechism, "Man's chief end is to glorify God, and to enjoy him forever," www.thewestminsterstandard.org/westminster-shorter-catechism/.

4. Roose, "An A.I.-Generated Picture Won."

5. Sherry Turkle, *Alone Together: Why We Expect More from Technology and Less from Each Other* (New York: Basic Books, 2011), 1.

6. Philosopher Richard Purtill defines a miracle as "an event in which God temporarily makes an exception to the natural order of things, to show that God is acting." Richard L. Purtill, "Defining Miracles," in *In Defense of Miracles: A Comprehensive Case for God's Action in History*, eds. R. Douglas Geivett and Gary R. Habermas (Downers Grove, IL: InterVarsity, 1997), 62–63.

7. Not only are they limited, but they also require ever-increasing maintenance. Just as "typing monkeys will never write 'Twelfth Night' without superhuman editors looking over their shoulders, so increasingly powerful artificial intelligences will require increasingly intensive human input and oversight.... [There is] a guiding principle that ... applies equally well to typing monkeys and today's language-learning models: 'Complex structures can only be generated by more complex structures.' Lacking constant curation, the result will be a procession of incoherent letters or what has come to be known as 'A.I. slop.'" Alexander Nazaryan, "Could Monkeys Really Type All of Shakespeare?" *New York Times*, January 3, 2025, www.nytimes.com/2025/01/03/science/monkeys-typewriter-shakespeare.html.

8. See Yoshua Bengio and Stuart J. Russell, interviews by Martin Ford, *Architects of Intelligence: The Truth about AI from the People Building It* (Birmingham, UK: Packt, 2018), 18–19 and 52–53.

9. Yuval Noah Harari, *Nexus: A Brief History of Information Networks from the Stone Age to AI* (New York: Random House, 2024), 209.

10. See Exodus 20:3–6; Psalm 115:4–8; Isaiah 42:17; 44:9–20; Jeremiah 11:12; Habakkuk 2:18; Romans 1:21–23; Galatians 4:8–9.

11. Andrea Long Chu, "My New Vagina Won't Make Me Happy and It Shouldn't Have To," *New York Times*, November 24, 2018, nytimes.com/2018/11/24/opinion/sunday/vaginoplasty-transgender-medicine.html.

12. Paul Kingsnorth, "Rage Against the Machine," *Free Press*, July 10, 2023, www.thefp.com/p/rage-against-the-machine-artificial-intelligence.

13. Karen Hao, "The Facebook Whistleblower Says Its Algorithms Are Dangerous. Here's Why," *MIT Technology Review*, October 5, 2021, www.technologyreview.com/2021/10/05/1036519/facebook-whistleblower-frances-haugen-algorithms/.

14. Tomas Chamorro-Premuzic, *I, Human: AI, Automation, and the Quest to Reclaim What Makes Us Unique* (Boston: Harvard Business Review, 2023), 71.

15. Chamorro-Premuzic, *I, Human*, 151.

16. Mary Harrington, "Soul Trader: Identity in a Digital Age," in *Identity in a Digital Age: A Pro-Human Vision for Technology*, eds. Benedict Rogers et al., (London: ARC Research, 2025), 9.

17. C. S. Lewis, *The Abolition of Man* (Oxford: Oxford University, 1943).

18. Stephen Prothero, *God Is Not One: The Eight Rival Religions That Run the World—and Why Their Differences Matter* (New York: HarperCollins, 2021), 11.

19. Elise Bohan, *Future Superhuman: Our Transhuman Lives in a Make-or-Break Century* (Sydney: NewSouth, 2022), 311.

20. Prothero, *God Is Not One*, 110.

21. Chamorro-Premuzic, *I, Human*, 18.

22. SXSW, "Martine Rothblatt: 'AI, Immortality and the Future of Selves,'" April 9, 2015, YouTube video, www.youtube.com/watch?v=5szXt6CBDmo.

23. SXSW, "Martine Rothblatt: 'AI, Immortality and the Future."

24. Jacob Shatzer, "Artificial Intelligence, Transhumanism, and the Question of the Person," in *Created in the Image of God: Applications and Implications for Our Cultural Confusion*, eds. David S. Dockery and Lauren McAfee (Nashville, TN: Forefront Books, 2023), 179.

25. See Thomas Nagel, "What Is It Like to Be a Bat?" *The Philosophical Review* 83, no. 4 (October 1974): 435–50, https://doi.org/10.2307/2183914.

26. Andrea Mew, "Facial Feminization Surgery Isn't Life-Saving, It Just Reinforces The So-Called 'Toxic Gender Binary,'" *Evie Magazine*, March 27, 2023, www.eviemagazine.com/post/facial-feminization-surgery-isnt-life-saving-reinforces-toxic-gender-binary.

27. See Ryan T. Anderson, *When Harry Became Sally: Responding to the Transgender Moment* (New York: Encounter, 2019), 104.

28. Katie J. McCoy, "What It Means to Be Male and Female," in Dockery and McAfee, *Created in the Image of God*, 151.

29. C. S. Lewis, *The Weight of Glory* (New York: HarperOne, 2001).

30. Stephen Witmer, "Wendell Berry and the Materiality of Creation," in *Creation and Doxology: The Beginning and End of God's Good World*, eds. Gerald Hiestand and Todd Wilson (Downers Grove, IL: InterVarsity, 2018), 123.

31. For more detail, see Gary Habermas, *On the Resurrection*, Vol. 1: Evidences (Brentwood, TN: B&H Academic, 2024); Habermas, *On the Resurrection*, Vol. 2: Refutations (Brentwood, TN: B&H Academic, 2024); Sean McDowell, *The Fate of the Apostles*, 2nd ed. (New York: Routledge, 2025); N. T. Wright, *The Resurrection of the Son of God* (Minneapolis, MN: Fortress, 2003); J. Warner Wallace, *Cold-Case Christianity, Updated & Expanded*, (Colorado Springs: David C Cook, 2023); Abdu Murray, "Is the Gospel of John Theological Fiction? With Dr. Lydia McGrew | Ep 63," Embrace the Truth podcast, August 26, 2024, https://embracethetruth.org/podcasts/is-the-gospel-of-john-theological-fiction-with-dr-lydia-mcgrew-ep-63/; Murray, "Maximal Data and the Gospels with Dr. Lydia McGrew | Ep 65," Embrace the Truth podcast, September 25, 2024,

https://embracethetruth.org/podcasts/maximal-data-gospels-lydia-mcgrew/.

32. Stanley Hauerwas and William H. Willimon, *The Truth about God: The Ten Commandments in Christian Life* (Nashville, TN: Abingdon, 1999), 68.

33. Clayton Kraby, "Why Is There Something Rather Than Nothing? Leibniz' Contingency Argument," *Reasonable Theology*, March 14, 2023, https://reasonabletheology.org/why-is-there-something-rather-than-nothing-leibniz-contingency-argument/.

34. Lewis, *The Weight of Glory*, 102.

35. Kelly M. Kapic, *You're Only Human: How Your Limits Reflect God's Design and Why That's Good News* (Grand Rapids, MI: Brazos, 2022), 12.

36. Kapic, *You're Only Human*, 102.

37. Paige Comstock Cunningham, "It All Begins in Genesis: Thinking Theologically about Medicine, Technology, and the Christian Life," in Hiestand and Wilson, *Creation and Doxology*, 174.

Chapter 9

1. Venki Ramakrishnan, "Will Computers Become Our Overlords?," in *Possible Minds: Twenty-Five Ways of Looking at AI*, ed. John Brockman (New York: Penguin Books, 2020), 190.

2. Ramakrishnan, "Will Computers Become Our Overlords?," 191.

3. Ramakrishnan, "Will Computers Become Our Overlords?," 191.

4. *Merriam-Webster*, s.v. "artificial (adj.)," accessed May 6, 2025, www.merriam-webster.com/dictionary/artificial.

5. Judea Pearl, "The Limitations of Opaque Learning Machines," in Brockman, *Possible Minds*, 16-17.

6. "Copyright Registration Guidance: Works Containing Material Generated by Artificial Intelligence," 88 Federal Register 16190, March 16, 2023, www.federalregister.gov/d/2023-05321/p-44.

7. Lucas Ropek, "Famous AI Artist Says He's Losing Millions of Dollars from People Stealing His Work," Gizmodo, October 1, 2024,

https://gizmodo.com/famous-ai-artist-says-hes-losing-millions-of-dollars-from-people-stealing-his-work-2000505822.

8. Tomas Chamorro-Premuzic, *I, Human: AI, Automation, and the Quest to Reclaim What Makes Us Unique* (Boston: Harvard Business Review, 2023), 119.

9. Stephen Wolfram, "Artificial Intelligence and the Future of Civilization," in Brockman, *Possible Minds*, 284.

10. Wolfram, "Artificial Intelligence," 284.

11. Thomas Nagel, *Mind and Cosmos: Why the Materialist Neo-Darwinian Conception of Nature Is Almost Certainly False* (New York: Oxford University, 2012), 8–12.

12. Closer To Truth, "Alexander Vilenkin—Is the Universe Fine-Tuned for Life and Mind?," January 23, 2024, YouTube video, www.youtube.com/watch?v=eLUj1WBW-Qk; Closer To Truth, "Roger Penrose—Is the Universe Fine-Tuned for Life and Mind?," August 20, 2019, YouTube video, www.youtube.com/watch?v=yDqny7UzyR4; Philip Goff, "Did the Dying Stephen Hawking Really Mean to Strengthen the Case for God?," *The Guardian*, May 7, 2018, www.theguardian.com/commentisfree/2018/may/07/stephen-hawking-god-multiverse-cosmology.

13. For substantive responses to the multiverse theory, see Gavin Ortlund, *Why God Makes Sense of a World That Doesn't: The Beauty of Christian Theism* (Grand Rapids, MI: Baker Academic, 2021), 64–69; Jeff Zweerink, *Escaping the Beginning? Confronting Challenges to the Universe's Origin* (Covina, CA: RTB Press, 2019), passim.

14. Francis Crick, *Life Itself: Its Origin and Nature* (New York: Simon and Schuster, 1981), 88.

15. Richard Dawkins, *River out of Eden: A Darwinian View of Life* (New York: Basic Books), 17; Bill Gates, *The Road Ahead*, rev. ed. (New York: Penguin, 1996), 188.

16. Stephen C. Meyer, *Darwin's Doubt: The Explosive Origin of Animal Life and the Case for Intelligent Design* (New York: HarperOne, 2013), 176–77.

17. Stephen C. Meyer, *Signature in the Cell: DNA and the Evidence for Intelligent Design* (New York: HarperCollins, 2009), 407.

18. "The Nobel Prize in Physiology or Medicine 2024," The Nobel Prize, October 7, 2024, www.nobelprize.org/prizes/medicine/2024/press-release/.

19. Fred Hoyle, "The Universe: Past and Present Reflections," *Annual Review of Astronomy and Astrophysics 20*, no. 1 (1982): 1–36.

20. Andy Crouch, "Intellectually Frustrated Atheists and Intellectually Frustrated Christians—The Strange Opportunity of the Late-Modern World," in *Creation and Doxology: The Beginning and End of God's Good World*, eds. Gerald Hiestand and Todd Wilson (Downers Grove, IL: InterVarsity, 2018), 154 (citing Robin Collins, "The Teleological Argument: An Exploration of the Fine-Tuning of the Universe," in *The Blackwell Companion to Natural Theology*, eds. William Lane Craig and J. P. Moreland [Chichester, England: Wiley-Blackwell, 2012]).

21. Nick Bostrom, "Are You Living in a Computer Simulation?," *Philosophical Quarterly* 53, no. 211 (2003): 243–55, https://simulation-argument.com/simulation/.

22. Rich McCormick, "Odds Are We're Living in a Simulation, Says Elon Musk," *Verge*, June 2, 2016, www.theverge.com/2016/6/2/11837874/elon-musk-says-odds-living-in-simulation.

23. Zohar Ringel and Dmitry L. Kovrizhin, "Quantized Gravitational Responses, the Sign Problem, and Quantum Complexity," *Science Advances* 3, no. 9 (September 27, 2017), cited in Margi Murphy, "It's the Red Pill: Scientists Confirm We Are NOT Living in a Computer Simulation," *The Sun*, updated October 20, 2017, www.thesun.co.uk/tech/4594362/are-we-living-in-a-computer-simulation/.

24. Crouch, "Intellectually Frustrated Atheists," 155.

25. Meghan O'Gieblyn, *God, Human, Animal, Machine: Technology, Metaphor, and the Search for Meaning* (New York: Anchor Books, 2022), 46–47.

26. O'Gieblyn, *God, Human, Animal, Machine*, 46.

27. Crouch, "Intellectually Frustrated Atheists," 152.

28. For a brief discussion of God's oneness accompanied by a list of Bible references that describe the Father as God, the Son as God, and the Holy Spirit as God, see Abdu Murray, *Grand Central Question: Answering the Critical Concerns of the Major Worldviews* (Downers Grove, IL: InterVarsity, 2014), 190–96.

Chapter 10

1. Richard Woods, ed., "Focus: Nature's Timebomb," *The Times* (UK), January 2, 2005, www.thetimes.com/uk/environment/article/focus-natures-timebomb-cbwdxwsd5xl?region=global.

2. Dominique Janicaud, *On the Human Condition* (New York: Routledge, 2005), 1, as quoted by Jens Zimmermann, *Incarnational Humanism: A Philosophy of Culture for the Church in the World* (Downers Grove, IL: InterVarsity, 2012), 22.

3. J. Scott Horrell, "'Persons' Divine and Human: The Concept for Person in and beyond Nicaea for Today," in *Created in the Image of God: Applications and Implications for Our Cultural Confusion*, eds. David S. Dockery and Lauren McAfee (Nashville, TN: Forefront Books, 2023), 57.

4. Mary Harrington, "Soul Trader: Identity in a Digital Age," in *Identity in a Digital Age: A Pro-Human Vision for Technology*, eds. Benedict Rogers et al., (London: ARC Research, 2025), 1.

5. See also Carl Trueman, *The Rise and Triumph of the Modern Self: Cultural Amnesia, Expressive Individualism, and the Road to Sexual Revolution* (Wheaton, IL: Crossway, 2020).

6. Harrington, "Soul Trader," 1.

7. Van Ethan Levy, "About Me," accessed March 30, 2025, https://vanethanlevy.com.

8. Interestingly, despite using the word *identity* synonymously with *person*, Levy published a blog entitled "Why the Term Transgender Is Transphobic," updated January 23, 2024, www.therapyroute.com/article/why-the-term-transition-is-transphobic-by-v-levy.

9. Jonathan Pageau, "Discovering Identity: Between Tyranny and Chaos," in Benedict Rogers et al., *Identity in a Digital Age*, 28.

10. Horrell, "'Persons' Divine and Human," in *Created in the Image of God*, 50.

11. Horrell, "'Persons' Divine and Human," 50.

12. C. Ben Mitchell, "What It Means to Be Human," in Dockery and McAfee, *Created in the Image of God*, 70–72.

13. Horrell, "'Persons' Divine and Human," 55.

14. Jacob Shatzer, "Artificial Intelligence, Transhumanism, and the Question of the Person," in Dockery and McAfee, *Created in the Image of God*, 180.

15. John F. Kilner, "The Image of God and Human Dignity: Recovering a Biblical Treasure," in Dockery and McAfee, *Created in the Image of God*, 23.

16. Kilner, "The Image of God and Human Dignity," 31.

17. Jens Zimmermann, *Incarnational Humanism: A Philosophy of Culture for the Church in the World* (Downers Grove, IL: InterVarsity, 2012), 40.

18. Horrell, "'Persons' Divine and Human," in *Created in the Image of God*, 65.

19. Horrell, "'Persons' Divine and Human," in *Created in the Image of God*, 61.

20. Kate Payne, "An AI Chatbot Pushed a Teen to Kill Himself, a Lawsuit against Its Creator Alleges," Associated Press, October 25, 2024, https://apnews.com/article/chatbot-ai-lawsuit-suicide-teen-artificial-intelligence-9d48adc572100822fdbc3c90d1456bd0.

21. Kaya Burgess, "Gen Z Half as Likely as Their Parents to Identify as Atheists," *The Times* (UK), January 25, 2025, www.thetimes.com/uk/religion/article/gen-z-half-as-likely-as-their-parents-to-identify-as-atheists-wp2vl0l29; Rikki Schlott, "Gen Z 'More Spiritual' than Millennials—Yet More Suspicious of Denominations," *New York Post*, May 27, 2023, https://nypost.com/2023/05/27/why-gen-z-is-more-spiritual-and-religious-than-millennials/.

22. See Harrington, "Soul Trader," 15.

23. Susan Harding, "Representing Fundamentalism: The Problem of the Repugnant Cultural Other," *Social Research* 58, no. 2 (Summer 1991); 373–93.

24. See Sam Allberry, *What God Has to Say about Our Bodies: How the Gospel Is Good News for Our Physical Selves* (Wheaton, IL: Crossway, 2021); Andrew T. Walker, *God and the Transgender Debate: What Does the Bible Actually Say about Gender Identity?* 2nd ed. (Epsom, UK: The Good Book Company, 2022); Robert S. Smith, *The Body God Gives: A Biblical Response to Transgender Theory* (Bellingham, WA: Lexham Academic, 2025); J. Alan Branch, *Affirming God's Image: Addressing the Transgender Question with Science and Scripture* (Bellingham, WA: Lexham, 2019).

25. Gregg R. Allison, "A Theology of Human Embodiment," in Dockery and McAfee, *Created in the Image of God*, 119.

26. Allison, "A Theology of Human Embodiment," 118.

27. Allison, "A Theology of Human Embodiment," 119.

28. Allison, "A Theology of Human Embodiment," 118.

29. Katie J. McCoy, "What It Means to Be Male and Female," in Dockery and McAfee, *Created in the Image of God*, 149.

30. *Batman Begins*, directed by Christopher Nolan (Burbank, CA: Warner Bros. Pictures, 2005).

31. Frank W. Boreham, "Our Rubbish Heaps," in *The Luggage of Life* (Grand Rapids, MI: Kregel, 1995), 147–54.

32. Boreham, "Our Rubbish Heaps," 147–54.

33. Mickey Badalamenti, "Kids on Swings," All Poetry, accessed March 29, 2025, allpoetry.com/poem/18076866-Kids-on-swings-by-M.-Badalamenti/, used with permission.

34. Kristen Deede Johnson, "Justice, Creation, and New Creation—In Christ All Things Hold Together," in *Creation and Doxology: The Beginning and End of God's Good World*, eds. Gerald Hiestand and Todd Wilson (Downers Grove, IL: InterVarsity, 2018), 197.

35. Johnson, "Justice, Creation, and New Creation," 197.

36. Kilner, "The Image of God and Human Dignity," 26.

37. Stephen Prothero, *God Is Not One: The Eight Rival Religions That Run the World—and Why Their Differences Matter* (New York: HarperCollins, 2021), 70–71.

38. C. Ben Mitchell, "What It Means to Be Human," 77.

39. Frank Boreham, *Mushrooms on the Moor* (Project Gutenberg, 2008), 4, www.gutenberg.org/ebooks/24134.

40. Richard Dawkins, "Atheists for Jesus?" *Free Inquiry*, December 2004/January 2005, https://cdn.centerforinquiry.org/wp-content/uploads/sites/26/2005/01/22160306/p09.pdf.

41. C. S. Lewis, *The Weight of Glory* (New York: HarperOne, 2001), 1–2.

Epilogue

1. Jonathan Haidt, *The Anxious Generation: How the Great Rewiring of Childhood Is Causing an Epidemic of Mental Illness* (New York: Penguin, 2024), 215.

2. Tara Isabella Burton, *Strange Rites: New Religions for a Godless World* (New York: PublicAffairs, 2023), 20–25, 45.